# Jane Austen's Table

*For my wonderful, beautiful mother, Carole Ann,*
*who loved Austen and good food alike.*

**Thunder Bay Press**
An imprint of Printers Row Publishing Group
9717 Pacific Heights Blvd, San Diego, CA 92121
www.thunderbaybooks.com • mail@thunderbaybooks.com

Copyright © Octopus Publishing Group, 2021
Text copyright © Robert Tuesley Anderson, 2021

Printers Row Publishing Group is a division of Readerlink Distribution Services, LLC.
Thunder Bay Press is a registered trademark of Readerlink Distribution Services, LLC.

Correspondence regarding the content of this book should be sent to Thunder Bay Press, Editorial Department, at the above address. Author and rights inquiries should be addressed to Pyramid, an imprint of Octopus Publishing Group Ltd., Carmelite House, 50 Victoria Embankment, London, EC4Y 0DZ
www.octopusbooks.co.uk

Thunder Bay Press
Publisher: Peter Norton • Associate Publisher: Ana Parker
Editor: Dan Mansfield
Acquisitions Editor: Kathryn Chipinka Dalby

Produced by Pyramid
Publisher: Lucy Pessell
Editor: Sarah Kennedy • Designer: Hannah Coughlin
Editorial Assistant: Emily Martin
Recipe Development: Jane Birch
Production Controllers: Nic Jones and Lucy Carter

Library of Congress Control Number: 2021938597

ISBN: 978-1-64517-913-9

Printed in China

26 25 24 23 22  3 4 5 6 7

# Jane Austen's Table

recipes inspired by the
works of Jane Austen

Robert Tuesley Anderson

THUNDER BAY
P·R·E·S·S

San Diego, California

# Contents

# Introduction

The characters in Jane Austen's novels belong to the well-to-do, leisured gentry and, even when thrown into straitened circumstances like the Dashwoods in *Sense and Sensibility* (1811), spend much of their time socializing—and, consequently, eating and drinking.

Alongside the everyday round of breakfasts, teas, and family dinners we find a profusion of more formal meals and "rout" suppers, and even—in perhaps the most famous scene in all of Austen—an idyllic summertime picnic. This last takes place in *Emma* (1815), where the whirl of social engagements and the meals that accompany them seem to preoccupy the characters more than in any of the other novels.

The food served up to us in the pages of Austen's fiction closely reflects the rich, heavy fare commonly eaten by the landed gentry in what can be loosely termed the Regency period (roughly 1795–1837). Ingredients were necessarily almost all local and seasonal, with the produce for the kitchen largely sourced from a surrounding estate or from an adjoining vegetable garden. More exotic foodstuffs like sugar, coffee, tea, chocolate, and spices as well as tropical fruits such as the pineapple were imported from the expanding British colonies but were, of course, expensive even for the rich.

The extravagance of the Georgian dinner table was only partly about sustenance; it was also—and especially in the context of entertaining—about status: the plain old showing off of wealth, consumption, and "good taste." The aspirational Mrs. Bennet in *Pride and Prejudice* (1813), a good few steps down in social rank than her new neighbor, Mr. Bingley, is at pains to show that her dinners are as good as, if not better than, his—despite (or because of!) the French-inflected pretensions of his cooks.

It is for social aperçus like this and to highlight her characters' foibles that Austen most often uses food in her novels. Meals and ingredients are rarely described sensually—Austen was no gourmand, no Regency Colette; she was, above all, a realist and describes food in a matter-of-fact way, even while freighting it with symbolic, ironic, or humorous meanings. Thus, when Emma Woodhouse, queen of the Highbury social scene, sends her rival, the slightly ailing Jane Fairfax, a packet of expensive "arrow-root" (which was used to make the jellies given to invalids), she is really drawing attention to her rival's subordinate, impoverished position, and when Miss Fairfax coolly sends back the same with "a thousand thanks," she is asserting her independence and her refusal to be patronized.

We do not have to rely only on the novels themselves when looking for evidence for how Austen and her contemporaries ate. The writer's surviving letters provide a rich treasure trove of domestic detail (we learn, for example, of Jane's role in making the family tea and cocoa in the morning) as do, crucially, the two surviving "receipt books" associated with the Austen family: one created by Martha Lloyd, who lived with Jane Austen and her mother and sister at their cottage in Chawton, and the rather grander one associated with Jane's brother, Edward Austen Knight, who owned the nearby landed estate, Chawton House. In addition, the Georgian period saw plenty of professionally published cookbooks, the most famous of which, Hannah Glasse's best-selling *The Art of Cookery Made Plain and Easy* (1747), was still widely in use in Austen's time.

In this book, we have mined all these sources to bring readers a sumptuous array of recipes that capture the spirit and verve of the food of Austen's world, but adapted and reimagined to suit our modern taste for lighter, healthier, more convenient dishes (Regency dishes were often labor- as well as calorie-intensive!). Here you will find modern recipes for everything from Mansfield Wood Roast Pheasant and Mary Musgrove's Meat Platter to Dr. Grant's Sandwiches, from General Tilney's Hot Chocolate to Rout Cake and Dowell Abbey Summer Berry Delice. The recipes are arranged according to the principal Georgian meals—breakfast and dinner—accompanied by additional chapters devoted to Nuncheons, Tidbits & Picnics; Ices, Cakes & Puddings; and Routs & Balls.

While we may not have the leisure, time, or money of an Emma, an Elizabeth, or even an Elinor to dine in truly "Jane Austen" style, a little of its opulence and a little of its romance can never really go amiss at our modern meals. This book will show you how.

# Breakfast

*There are very few breakfast scenes in Jane Austen's novels. Perhaps this was because of the novelist's sense of propriety; after all, breakfast was—and still is—the most intimate and private of meals, taken when a household was still in mufti, so to speak, not quite ready to face the day and for the round of visits and visitors this might entail.*

*While for most ordinary men and women of the Georgian period breakfast was often a hearty affair featuring bread, meat, and ale, eaten early to get the working day off to a good start and on a full stomach, for the gentry breakfast was typically much lighter and certainly more leisurely, taken as late as ten or eleven o'clock. In the cottage at Chawton, Hampshire—where Jane Austen wrote her last three novels—we know that the writer, her mother, and her sister ate little more than tea and toast for the meal, and that only after an hour or two of small chores, a short country walk, or even a round of letter writing. Jane Austen, for example, fitted in an hour's practice at the pianoforte before she set about making the family's tea.*

*Nonetheless, in grander homes, breakfast could become much more elaborate. At the pinnacle of the social hierarchy, the Prince Regent's favorite breakfast consisted of two pigeons and three beefsteaks, washed down with white wine, a glass of dry Champagne, two glasses of port, and a glass of brandy. There was such a thing as a compromise: during a visit to a wealthy relative, Jane Austen's mother wrote a letter praising the elegance of the breakfast table, which featured "Chocolate Coffee and Tea, Plumb Cake, Pound Cake, Hot Rolls, Cold Rolls, Bread and Butter." It is such elegance that is the watchword in the recipes here.*

# Henry Crawford's Lazy Breakfast Eggs

This slow cooker recipe is ideal for a leisurely Sunday breakfast. It's quick to prepare: just pop everything in the slow cooker and leave it to cook gently while you read the papers and drink a cup of coffee.

———————————————

*T*he supremely health-conscious Mr. Woodhouse's advice to the elderly Mrs. Bates in Emma is somewhat in line with our attitude to eggs today—they are good for you when eaten in moderation.

*"Mrs. Bates, let me propose your venturing on one of these eggs. An egg boiled very soft is not unwholesome. Serle understands boiling an egg better than any body. I would not recommend an egg boiled by any body else; but you need not be afraid, they are very small, you see—one of our small eggs will not hurt you."*

*The following recipe, then, is a late Sunday morning treat. Imagine the rakish Henry Crawford, the antihero of* Mansfield Park *and Fanny's suitor, having risen late after a Saturday night on the town, sitting down to this hearty meal, prepared by his cook or manservant. Perfect washed down with another raffish delight, Frank Churchill's Cardamom Coffee.*

## SERVES 4

PREP + COOKING TIME:
   55 MINUTES

2 tablespoons butter
4 thin slices of honey roast ham
4 teaspoons spicy tomato chutney
4 eggs
2 cherry tomatoes, halved
1 scallion, finely sliced
salt and black pepper
4 slices of buttered toast, to serve

1. Preheat the slow cooker. Use a little of the butter to grease four ½-cup ovenproof dishes (checking first that the dishes fit in your slow cooker pot). Press a slice of ham into each dish to line the base and sides, leaving a small overhang of ham above the dish.

2. Place 1 teaspoon of chutney in the base of each dish, then break an egg on top. Add a cherry tomato half to each, sprinkle with the scallion, season to taste, then dot with the remaining butter. Cover the tops with greased foil and put in the slow cooker pot.

3. Pour boiling water into the slow cooker pot to come halfway up the sides of the dishes, cover, and cook on high for 40–50 minutes or until the egg whites are set and the yolks still slightly soft.

4. Remove the foil and gently run a round-bladed knife between the ham and the edges of the dishes. Turn out and quickly turn the baked eggs the right way up. Place each on a plate and serve with the buttered toast, cut into fingers.

# Mrs. Cassandra Austen's Scrambled Eggs

This indulgent version of scrambled eggs, served on rich brioche and enhanced with light cream and goat's cheese, is a lovely breakfast treat, and is delicious as it is or served with some asparagus on the side.

---

*I*n Jane Austen's time, it was common for farms, cottages, and other rural dwellings to include a poultry yard. Generally under the supervision of the mistress of the house, home-reared poultry played a vital role in a household's economy, providing not only fresh eggs but the occasional chicken (or turkey, etc.) for the pot. Jane's mother, Cassandra Leigh Austen (1739–1827), ran such a yard at her husband's parsonage in Steventon, Hampshire, where the author grew up, and later, from 1809, she had another at the cottage at Chawton, where she and her daughters finally found a settled home after the death of the Rev. George Austen. Her yard would have included ducks as well as hens, and possibly geese and turkeys, too. In Emma, Mrs. Weston, the heroine's erstwhile governess, runs just such a well-stocked yard—until, that is, it is pilfered, not by foxes but "by the ingenuity of man."

*While Mrs. Austen and her daughters usually ate only a very modest breakfast, we might like to imagine her asking her cook to rustle up some nicely buttered fresh-laid eggs when one of her sons paid her a visit.*

## SERVES 2

PREP + COOKING TIME:
15 MINUTES

4 slices of brioche, toasted

4 large eggs

4 tablespoons light cream

1 cup asparagus spears, woody ends removed

1 tablespoon butter

⅓ cup soft goat cheese, diced

salt and black pepper

1. Lightly toast the brioche slices under a preheated broiler until just golden, then turn over and lightly toast on the other side. Keep warm.

2. Beat the eggs and cream together in a bowl and season with salt and pepper.

3. Steam the asparagus spears for 4–5 minutes until tender.

4. Meanwhile, melt the butter in a small saucepan, add the egg mixture, and cook over a low heat, stirring with a wooden spoon, until softly set. Remove from the heat and stir in the goat cheese.

5. Serve the scrambled eggs on the toasted brioche with the steamed asparagus alongside.

# Oatmeal

Beginning the day with a steaming bowl of nutritious oatmeal (or gruel, as it is referred to in Austen's works) will get you off to a flying start. It's packed with antioxidants, fiber, and vitamins. You can vary the toppings that you add for extra flavor and an added health boost.

*W*hen Isabella, the elder daughter of Mr. Woodhouse, arrives at her father's home, Hartfield, after traveling down from London with her husband and five children, exhausted and no doubt fractious, his immediate advice seems rather odd: "You must go to bed early, my dear—and I recommend a little gruel to you before you go—you and I will have a nice basin of gruel together." In the fictional village of Highbury where everyone else seems more than ready to tuck into all manner of pies and puddings, Emma's sentimental, hypochondriacal father strikes a rare note of abstemiousness: for every condition and for every constitution, his enduring dietary advice is gruel—the blend of oats and water and/or milk we better know as oatmeal.

*Gruel made simply with oats and water was primarily the food of the poor (it would become the chief sustenance of the Victorian workhouse) as well as the invalid, and could be served at any time of day. We, however, prefer to make it for breakfast with milk, perhaps with a topping of Donwell Abbey Strawberry Conserve or—a Regency favorite—dried or fresh fruit. Try not to think of Mr. Woodhouse tut-tutting from the other side of the breakfast table, though!*

## SERVES 4–6

PREP + COOKING TIME: 15 MINUTES

5 cups milk
generous 2 cups water
1 teaspoon vanilla extract
pinch of ground cinnamon
pinch of salt
2 cups rolled oats

*For the toppings*
Donwell Abbey Strawberry Conserve
   (see page 21)
honey or maple syrup and chopped
   nuts
fresh berries
chopped banana, raisins, and a
   sprinkle of ground nutmeg
pear slices and a pinch of ground
   ginger

1. Put the milk, water, vanilla extract, cinnamon, and salt in a large saucepan over a medium heat and bring slowly to a boil.

2. Stir in the oats, then reduce the heat and simmer gently, stirring occasionally, for 8–10 minutes until creamy and tender.

3. Spoon the oatmeal into individual bowls and serve with the toppings of your choice.

# The Comtesse de Feullide's Breakfast Brioches Three Ways

Enriched with eggs and butter, brioche is the prince of breads and very versatile, as these three breakfast recipes show. Enjoy it with vanilla-flecked mascarpone and raspberries, piled high with creamy mushrooms, or turned into that breakfast favorite, French toast.

*J*ane's cousin, and later sister-in-law and friend, Eliza Capot, Comtesse de Feullide (1761–1813), was something of an exotic specimen and interloper in the novelist's quiet country circles. Born in India, as a young woman she settled in France and married a French count and army captain who, in the wake of the French Revolution of 1789, was arrested and guillotined for conspiracy against the new regime. Eliza returned to England, where her visits to the country parsonage in Steventon had a lively impact on the young Jane Austen and her siblings; she would eventually marry Austen's favorite brother, Henry. She played the harp, wore fashionable clothes, loved to ride, and had a partiality for theatricals, always, of course, taking the part of the leading lady.

*No doubt, too, Eliza had a taste for Frenchified delicacies, including, perhaps, the butter-and-egg-rich breads known as brioches that were sometimes eaten at breakfast in the best houses of Regency England. Eliza's vivacious, slight "fast" character had an enduring impact on her cousin's work—from the calculating heroine of the novel-in-letters* Lady Susan *(written 1795 and first published in 1871) to mature works such as* Mansfield Park, *where the charming but worldly Mary Crawford bears more than a passing resemblance to Austen's sister-in-law. Here, we have come up with two different wonderfully wicked brioche variations named for these characters.*

*Continued* ⇀

# Lady Susan's Raspberry and Mascarpone Brioche

## SERVES 4

PREP + COOKING TIME: 10 MINUTES

4 slices of brioche
1 cup raspberries

*For the vanilla mascarpone*

1¼ cups mascarpone cheese
2 tablespoons light cream
seeds from 1 vanilla bean
1–2 tablespoons confectioners' sugar,
   plus extra to dust

1. Make the vanilla mascarpone. Stir the mascarpone, cream, vanilla seeds, and confectioners' sugar together until smooth—do not overbeat.

2. Toast the brioche slices under a medium broiler for 30 seconds on each side until lightly browned. Top with the raspberries and vanilla mascarpone and dust with confectioners' sugar.

# Mary Crawford's Tarragon & Mushroom Brioche

## SERVES 4

PREP + COOKING TIME: 20 MINUTES

8 slices of brioche
1½ sticks butter
2 banana shallots, finely chopped
3 garlic cloves, finely chopped
4 cups sliced mixed wild mushrooms
4 tablespoons sour cream, plus extra
   to serve (optional)
2 tablespoons finely chopped
   tarragon
1 tablespoon finely chopped
   Italian parsley
salt and black pepper

1. Toast the brioche slices under a medium broiler for 30 seconds on each side until lightly browned. Keep warm.

2. Heat the butter in a skillet and sauté the shallots and garlic for 1–2 minutes. Add the mushrooms and stir-fry over a medium heat for 6–8 minutes. Season well, remove from the heat, and stir in the sour cream and chopped herbs.

3. Spoon the mushrooms onto the toasted brioche and serve immediately, with an extra dollop of sour cream if desired.

# Love and Friendship Pain Perdu

**W**ritten *when Jane Austen was just 14, the hilarious* Love and Friendship *is, with its unlikely adventures and swooning heroines, a pastiche of the eighteenth-century romantic novel. Austen wrote it to entertain her family but fittingly dedicated it to her exotic, cosmopolitan cousin, Eliza, Comtesse de Feullide, then newly arrived from revolutionary France, alongside the epigraph: "Deceived in Friendship and Betrayed in Love."*

## SERVES 4

PREP + COOKING TIME: **20** MINUTES

4 thick slices of brioche
2 eggs
6 tablespoons milk
3½ tablespoons butter
¾ cup yogurt
2 cups raspberries
¾ cup blueberries
confectioners' sugar, for dusting, or
    maple syrup

1. Cut the brioche into triangles. Beat the eggs and milk in a shallow bowl with a fork.

2. Heat half the butter in a skillet. Dip each triangle into the egg mixture, then transfer to the skillet. Cook over a medium heat until the underside is golden. Turn over and repeat, then lift out of the skillet and keep hot.

3. Heat the remaining butter in the skillet, and dip and cook the remaining brioche triangles.

4. Serve two triangles topped with a spoonful of yogurt, a sprinkling of berries, and a light dusting of sifted confectioners' sugar or a drizzle of maple syrup. Serve immediately.

# Donwell Abbey Strawberry Conserve

This unusual fresh strawberry conserve is super-easy to make—no boiling or endless stirring needed here!—and perfect atop hot buttered toast and crusty bread, or on Oatmeal (page 14).

---

*D*uring *his summer party in* Emma, *Mr. Knightley happily exclaims to his guests, "Come, and eat my strawberries. They are ripening fast." The strawberry, with its full heart shape and rich red color, has long had associations with love and passion (it was sacred to the Greek goddess Aphrodite), and—if we did not know the rather staid, respectable hero of Austen's novel better—we might think his invitation a rather flirtatious one. It certainly proves alluring to Mr. Knightley's guests who, led by the rector's wife, Mrs. Elton, are soon busy gathering, as she says, "the best fruit in England—every body's favorite—always wholesome."*

*With so many eager gatherers, we may well wonder what happened that day to the surplus of fresh-picked fruit from Donwell Abbey's famous strawberry beds. Perhaps Mr. Knightley's cook made it into a simple, summer-tasting conserve just like this one.*

## MAKES 6 POTS

PREP TIME: 20 MINUTES, PLUS
    STANDING AND FREEZING

4 cups strawberries, hulled and sliced

5 cups superfine sugar

4 tablespoons freshly squeezed lemon
   juice (about 2 lemons)

⅔ cup liquid pectin

1. Crush the strawberries with a potato masher, or by blending briefly in a food processor using the pulse setting so that there are pieces of strawberry rather than a fine purée. Add to a large bowl and stir in the sugar, then cover and leave to stand for 1½–2 hours, stirring from time to time, until the sugar has dissolved.

2. Stir in the lemon juice, then add the pectin and continue stirring for 2 minutes. Ladle into small, clear plastic pots, leaving a gap of ½ inch at the top. Clip or press on lids. Label and leave at room temperature overnight for the conserve to "gel."

3. Transfer to the freezer to store until required. Thaw overnight in the refrigerator, then transfer to attractive jars and serve in the same way as a conventional jelly.

# Bath Buns

These traditional sweet rolls with their crushed sugar cube topping are best served on the day they are made—better still, warm from the oven. Split and spread with butter or, for a special treat, top each half with thick whipped cream and strawberry preserve.

## MAKES 12

PREP + COOKING TIME: 1 HOUR
  PLUS PROOFING

2¼ teaspoons active dry yeast

1 cup milk, heated until warm

3⅔ cups white bread flour, plus extra
  for dusting

⅓ cup superfine sugar

1 teaspoon sea salt

2 sticks butter

1 cup golden raisins

1 large egg, beaten

*For the topping*

1 tablespoon milk

2 tablespoons superfine sugar

4 white sugar cubes, lightly crushed

1. Whisk the yeast into the milk and set aside. Combine the flour, sugar, and sea salt in a large bowl. Using your fingertips, rub in the butter until the mixture is like fine bread crumbs.

2. With a wooden spoon, stir in the milk mixture until well combined. It will appear a bit wet, but don't add any flour. Rest the dough for 10 minutes.

3. Turn onto a floured surface and knead well for 8–10 minutes until the dough becomes more elastic. Place in a large clean bowl, cover with a clean damp dish towel, and leave in a warm place for 1½ hours, or until doubled in size.

4. Turn the dough out onto a lightly floured work surface. Roughly flatten it, then sprinkle with the golden raisins and quickly work them in. Divide into 12 equal pieces and roll into balls. Place well apart on a nonstick cookie sheet and cover with a damp dish towel.

5. Leave in a warm place for 30 minutes, or until doubled in size, then brush the tops of the buns with the beaten egg. Bake at 375°F for 15–20 minutes or until golden and they sound hollow when tapped underneath.

6. While the buns are baking, warm the milk and sugar for the topping in a small saucepan over a low heat until the sugar has dissolved.

7. Transfer the buns to a wire rack and brush generously with the milk mixture while still hot, then sprinkle with the crushed sugar cubes.

*T*hese sugar-crusted sweet buns are familiar to anyone who visits the Regency city of Bath, and seem to have been made there, in one form or another, since the mid-eighteenth century. Their supposed creator was the celebrated physician of the city Dr. William Oliver (1695–1764), who "prescribed" them to his patients. When this diet proved—we are shocked and surprised to learn—too fattening for some, he came up with another recipe, for the dry, buttery cookies or crackers that are still marketed today under the name of "Bath Olivers."

Both the buns and cookies were famous in the eighteenth century. After the doctor's death, his coachman set up a shop in Bath to sell the cookies, and recipes for the Bath bun abounded in published cookbooks. The original Bath bun was sprinkled with caraway confits—sugar-coated caraway seeds—at least according to a recipe published in The Experienced English Housekeeper (1769), by Elizabeth Raffald, who advises her readers, rather cozily, to "send them in hot for breakfast."

Jane Austen had more than a passing acquaintance with this sweet treat, if a letter to her sister, Cassandra, written from an aunt's home in Bath, is anything to go by. Though kindly, her aunt, Jane Leigh-Perrot, was somewhat mean when it came to household expenses, and Jane quips to her sister that she will have to make herself a cheap guest by "disordering my stomach with Bath buns"—perhaps not quite the effect Dr. Oliver had been after!

# Lady Catherine de Bourgh's Caraway and Raisin Breakfast Bread

One for the grown-ups—it contains beer, so isn't suitable for children—this deliciously moist loaf has a hint of licorice from the caraway seeds. It's perfect sliced and buttered, then served with piping-hot coffee or tea for a weekend brunch.

*F*ruited and spiced breads were a popular addition to the breakfast tables of the wealthy. Here we have come up with a recipe good enough to serve at Rosings Park, the luxurious home of Mr. Darcy's pompous, arrogant aunt, Lady Catherine de Bourgh—one of the most memorable antagonists in Austen's novels. No doubt her "patronee," Mr. Collins, would think it the finest fruited bread in England.

## SERVES 10

PREP + COOKING TIME: 1 HOUR 10 MINUTES, PLUS STANDING

1 cup raisins
1¼ cups beer
¾ cup dark brown sugar
1 teaspoon caraway seeds
1 egg, beaten
scant 1½ cups self-rising flour
1¼ cups whole-wheat flour
1 teaspoon baking powder

1. Put the raisins and beer in a small saucepan and bring just to a boil, then remove from the heat. Pour into a large bowl and leave to stand until cold.

2. Stir the sugar, caraway seeds, and egg into the beer mixture. Add the flours and baking powder and stir in.

3. Spoon the mixture into a greased and lined 8 x 4-inch loaf pan and spread into the corners. Bake at 350°F for about 50 minutes until risen, firm to the touch, and a skewer inserted into the center comes out clean. Loosen the bread at the ends and transfer to a wire rack. Peel off the lining paper and leave to cool.

# Pound Cake

Delicious any time of day, this cake is especially good for breakfast, topped with strawberries or raspberries. A spin on the classic recipe, it's enhanced with the flavors of orange and star anise.

*A*s its name implies, the pound cake originally featured an extravagant pound each of eggs, butter, sugar, and flour. This being before the days of chemical raising agents, the cook would spend a lot of time beating air into the eggs and slowly folding in the rest of the ingredients, to ensure that the baked cake would be as light and airy as possible. That said, a pound cake from Jane Austen's time would still have been rather dense and heavy in comparison to its modern counterpart, so its name seems doubly apposite.

It is doubtless to pound cake that Austen is referring when she remarked, in a 1808 letter to her sister, Cassandra: "You know how interesting the purchase of a sponge-cake is to me." Knowing the author's penchant for irony—and, indeed, downright sarcasm—this most likely was meant as a jibe at the expense of some rich acquaintance who could afford to buy such a cake rather than having it made at home, as would have happened in the Austens' more straitened household.

## SERVES 10

PREP + COOKING TIME: 1 HOUR

4 star anise, broken into pieces

generous ¾ cup superfine sugar

1¾ sticks butter, softened

3 eggs

finely grated zest of 1 orange

2 tablespoons orange juice

2 cups self-rising flour

1 teaspoon baking powder

small piece of candied orange zest, cut
    into thin strips

*To decorate*

5 oz. lemon curd

½ cup sour cream

fresh berries or crystallized rose
    petals (optional)

1. Put the star anise and a quarter cup of the sugar in a small food processor, blender, or coffee grinder and grind until the star anise is completely ground.

2. Tip into a bowl, add the butter, remaining sugar, eggs, orange zest and juice, flour, and baking powder, and beat together until pale and creamy. Spoon the mixture into a greased and lined 7-inch round cake pan and level the surface.

3. Place the strips of candied zest on the center of the cake. Bake at 325°F for about 50 minutes or until just firm to the touch and a skewer inserted into the center comes out clean. Loosen the edge, turn out onto a wire rack, and peel off the lining paper.

4. Mix the lemon curd and sour cream together and spread over the top of the cake. Sprinkle with crystallized rose petals or flowers, if using.

# Frank Churchill's Cardamom Coffee

Redolent with the exotic scent and subtle flavor of cardamom, this takes your morning cup of coffee to a whole new level and is definitely worth the effort. It's delicious with a slice of sticky Gingerbread Loaf (page 133).

*M*iss Bates's decided preference for tea over coffee in Emma was a common one among Regency women: "No coffee, I thank you, for me—never take coffee. A little tea if you please, sir, by and bye..." Coffee, while widely consumed, could never quite throw off its associations with the ubiquitous coffeehouses of the eighteenth century—where mostly men gathered to read newspapers, do deals, and discuss the politics of the day. Coffee was masculine, rakish, and even seditious, and kept men away from their homes and families. No wonder the socially nervous, if endlessly talkative, Miss Bates seems to show a certain squeamishness toward it and a liking for the much more genteel and domestic tea. By contrast, her niece Jane Fairfax's secret fiancé, Frank Churchill—a man about town if ever there was one—would have been a great coffee drinker, we imagine. In the following recipe the addition of cardamom—a spice, incidentally, often used as a breath freshener in Jane Austen's day—adds another touch of exotic decadence to the drink.

## SERVES 4

PREP + COOKING TIME: 10 MINUTES

4 cups water

4 cardamom pods

4 teaspoons very finely ground
   Arabica coffee

4 teaspoons sugar

1. Place the measured water and cardamom pods in a small saucepan and carefully spoon the coffee and sugar on top. Gently stir the sugar and coffee into the surface of the water, making sure you don't touch the bottom of the pan with the spoon.

2. Bring to just below boiling point over a medium heat, gradually drawing in the outer edges of the coffee into the middle to create a froth. Just as the coffee is about to bubble, spoon some of the froth into four coffee cups and pour in the coffee. Leave to stand for 1 minute before drinking to let the coffee grains settle at the bottom of the cups.

# General Tilney's Hot Chocolate

A hug in a mug on a cold day and heaven for chocolate lovers, this velvety hot chocolate is finished off with a luxurious whipped Irish cream for an extra kick. Omit the liqueur and top with marshmallows if you prefer.

———————————————•———————————————

*I*n Northanger Abbey—*Austen's satire of Gothic fiction with its remote, sinister castles and dark mysteries—the "villain" of the plot, General Tilney, for all his machinations, is portrayed as being no more than an urbane man of fashion whose only interest is swelling his family's coffers. Austen deftly brings him down to size by depicting him enjoying hot cocoa at the breakfast table, but selfishly not offering it to either his daughter or his guest, the "heroine," Catherine Morland.*

*Hot cocoa, made at first with water and later with milk, became extremely popular in Georgian England, served in coffeehouses and even chocolate houses—hothouses both of social networking and political and intellectual debate. In the domestic setting, cocoa was often boiled up at the table in a samovar-like pot over a flame, often sweetened and spiced. It could be drunk, of course, at any time of day.*

*The following recipe is just as the villainous general likes it: not too rich, but gently spiced. Be sure to share it with your fellow breakfasters, though!*

## SERVES 4

PREP + COOKING TIME: **10** MINUTES

7 oz. coarsely grated dark chocolate, plus extra for sprinkling

3¾ cups milk

⅔ cup heavy cream

1 tablespoon confectioners' sugar

⅓ cup Irish cream liqueur (optional)

1–2 tablespoons superfine sugar, according to taste

1. Place the chocolate in a large heatproof jug. Heat the milk in a pan until it is almost simmering.

2. Meanwhile, whip the heavy cream with the confectioners' sugar until it forms soft peaks, then fold in 1 tablespoon of the cream liqueur if using.

3. Pour about a quarter of the hot milk into the jug, stirring until the chocolate has melted. Add the remaining milk in a steady stream, stirring constantly. Add the remaining Irish cream and sweeten to taste with the superfine sugar.

4. Pour the hot chocolate into mugs and top with the desired quantity of whipped cream. Sprinkle with a little extra grated chocolate to decorate, and serve immediately.

# Food and Austen's Flourishing Heroines

Good health and a healthy appetite go hand in hand in Austen's novels. Her heroines—when flourishing—eat in moderation and without worrying too much about what they are eating and what they are not. Catherine Morland, the youthful, zestful heroine of Northanger Abbey, is blessed with "a good appetite" and eats just what she wants to, when she is hungry. The heroines' good constitutions—and well-regulated appetites—are also conjoined with a taste for fresh air and exercise. Often, they are determined walkers, visiting friends and neighbors on foot, enjoying scenic strolls (Catherine) or traipsing, like the best of the Romantics, through the natural world (Marianne Dashwood). Elizabeth Bennet thinks nothing of walking three miles "in [...] dirty weather" to see her cold-ridden sister marooned at Netherfield, "crossing field after field at a quick pace, jumping over stiles and springing over puddles with impatient activity, and finding herself at last within view of the house, with weary ankles, dirty stockings, and a face glowing with the warmth of exercise."

We might go so far to claim that appetite, exercise, and mental health are the three points of a Jane Austen "well-being triangle"—if any one of these is lost, the others suffer, too, and overall well-being is compromised. When out of sorts, her heroines begin to display a more problematic relationship with food. For example, when Marianne in Sense and Sensibility begins to pine for Willoughby, her appetite dwindles and she becomes thin and wan, losing her youthful bloom. Catherine, too, loses her appetite when she finds she is banished from Northanger Abbey—"She tried to eat [...] but she had no appetite, and could not swallow many mouthfuls"—a situation that continues back at home where she appears—from her parents' point of view—to turn her nose up at their ordinary breakfast: "I am sure I do not care about the bread. It is all the same to me what I eat." While both Elizabeth Bennet and Emma Woodhouse—both of whom have healthy egos to match their healthy appetites—flourish throughout their respective narratives, two others, Anne Elliot (in Persuasion) and Fanny Price (in Mansfield Park)—each unhappy and marginalized in her own way—have to work their way toward well-being, rediscovering their appetites (in the broadest sense) along with their sense of self as they also begin to (re-)bloom physically and emotionally.

Austen's concern with food and flourishing is played out negatively in her supporting characters. In contrast to her flourishing heroines, those characters whom we are asked to look at critically are shown to have an unbalanced relationship with food. On the one hand, she shows us individuals (mostly men) who overengage with food, giving it too much importance in their daily lives. Such is Mr. Hurst in Pride and Prejudice who, Elizabeth discovers when sitting next to him at dinner, "lived only to eat, drink, and play at cards" and "who, when he found her to prefer a plain dish to a ragout, had nothing to say to her." Likewise, the cossetted, overweight Arthur Parker in Sanditon is unhealthily preoccupied with hot chocolate and buttered toast.

Obsessiveness with food can go the other way—a neurotic concern with the effects of (too much) food on health. Here the classic portrait in Austen is Emma's father, Mr. Woodhouse, whose main trait, in fact, is his endless fussing about not only what he is eating but what those around him are eating, too. Gruel (the invalid's diet) is, for him, the perfect foodstuff—recommended to all and sundry, whatever their state of health. He has an opinion on the healthiness of every item from "unwholesome preserves" to wedding cake. There is plenty of affection shown in the novel for Mr. Woodhouse—reflecting Emma's own—but his food obsession is shown to be a disorder, the inevitable consequence of a life spent too much cooped indoors and pampered.

Austen's message in her novels—of having a good appetite spurred on by exercise but all the while disentangling appetite from emotion—is a challenging one, but remains relevant to our human flourishing today.

# Picnics, Nuncheons

# & Other Light Meals

*T*here were plenty of other opportunities for eating and drinking in the Regency period outside the principal meals of breakfast and dinner. Lunch, however—as least as this term is understood today—was not one of them. The gentry ate their breakfast so late that a midday meal of any size would have been redundant (or just plain greedy).

The term "luncheon" or "nuncheon" existed but, according to the eighteenth-century lexicographer Samuel Johnson, was not much more than a snack. Luncheon *in his famous dictionary is defined* "as much food as one's hand can hold"—perhaps a hunk of bread and cheese or meat (which in the late eighteenth century became known as a "sandwich"), washed down with a flagon of beer. We find comparable light meals in Austen's novels: thus, the languorous Mary Musgrove, in Persuasion, *is persuaded to stir herself from her sofa to eat a bit of cold meat before going out on a "little" afternoon walk.*

More elaborate food was occasionally eaten in the middle of the day—notably during the picnics that became highly fashionable during the Regency period (in London there was even a Picnic Society). While the picnic was borrowed from France, in Britain it was given additional impetus owing to the cult of the "picturesque"—the seeking out and depiction of idyllic landscape views. The western slope of Box Hill in Surrey—the setting of the grand picnic in Emma—was just such a view.

Here we invite you to—among other things—try out a country picnic Jane Austen style, but politely suggest you refrain from making fun of your guests as Emma makes fun of poor Miss Bates.

# Box Hill Picnic Pies

Summertime means picnic time, so add these Mediterranean-style veg-filled pies, with their unusual cheesy pastry, to your portable feast. They're equally delicious warm or cold, so spread out that picnic blanket and tuck in.

## MAKES 4

PREP + COOKING TIME: 1 HOUR

1 tablespoon olive oil

1 onion, chopped

2 garlic cloves, finely chopped

1 zucchini, diced

½ yellow bell pepper, deseeded and diced

½ red bell pepper, deseeded and diced

14-oz. can chopped tomatoes

1 tablespoon chopped rosemary or basil

½ teaspoon superfine sugar

beaten egg, to glaze

salt and black pepper

*For the pastry*

scant 1½ cups bread flour

5 tablespoons butter, diced

1 cup diced mature cheddar cheese, plus extra, shredded, for sprinkling

2 egg yolks

2 teaspoons water

1. Heat the oil in a saucepan, add the onion, and fry for 5 minutes until softened. Add the garlic, zucchini, and diced bell peppers and fry briefly, then add the tomatoes, herbs, sugar, and a little salt and pepper. Simmer, uncovered, for 10 minutes, stirring from time to time until thickened. Cool.

2. Make the pastry. Add the flour, butter, and a little salt and pepper to a bowl, rub in the butter until you have fine crumbs, then stir in the cheese. Add the egg yolks and water and mix to form a smooth dough.

3. Knead lightly, then cut the dough into four pieces. Roll one of the pieces out between two sheets of plastic wrap, patting into a neat shape until you have a 7-inch circle. Remove the top sheet of plastic wrap, spoon a fourth of the filling in the center, brush the pastry edges with beaten egg, then fold the pastry circle in half while still on the lower piece of plastic wrap.

4. Peel the pastry off the wrap, lift onto an oiled baking sheet, press the edges together well, and press together any breaks in the pastry. Repeat with the remaining pastry pieces and filling until four pies have been made.

5. Brush with beaten egg, sprinkle with a little shredded cheese, and bake at 375°F for 20 minutes until golden brown. Loosen and transfer to a wire rack to cool.

*B*ox Hill in Surrey—the setting for the most famous scene in Emma—was already a popular attraction for visitors in the seventeenth century, famous for the box woodlands that had been planted there from medieval times and which gave it its name. The diarist and gardener John Evelyn (1620–1706) visited the hill in 1655, and wrote admiringly of "those natural bowers, cabinets and shady walks in the box copses," but by Jane Austen's time—with the rise of the fashion for the picturesque and scenic touring—it was as much the views from the hill as the hill itself that drew the crowds of sightseers.

Today a large part of the hill is owned and managed by the British organization the National Trust, the box plantations still thrive, and the views remain spectacular. Modern-day visitors might do no better than to take along these Mediterranean-inspired picnic pies to munch upon as they drink in the natural wonders.

# Elizabeth Martin's Sausage Rolls

Who doesn't love a sausage roll, especially at a picnic? This recipe takes an old favorite and gives it extra zing by adding fiery harissa paste and fresh ginger. They'll be gone in minutes!

*While the principal characters in Jane Austen's novels are largely drawn from the country gentry among whom she grew up, she nonetheless sometimes offers sympathetic portraits of those lower down the social scale. Perhaps the most sympathetically drawn are the Martins in Emma—the well-to-do tenant farmer Robert Martin and his sister Elizabeth—who, for all the heroine's snobbery toward them, are consistently shown as sensible, right-thinking, and kind—providing an unflattering foil for the often vain and frivolous Highbury set, of which Emma is the lynchpin. Robert Martin is the perfect suitor for Emma's protégée, Harriet Smith (we might even think he deserves a lot better!), though it's not until toward the end of the book that Emma finally recognizes it.*

*Let's imagine an alternative, happier, more harmonious party to Box Hill, hosted by the Martins, at which good honest food is served, cooked by Elizabeth Martin using produce from her brother's farm and her own kitchen garden. The stars of her picnic basket might be these delicious ginger-spiked sausage rolls.*

## MAKES 30

PREP + COOKING TIME: **50** MINUTES

1 lb. good-quality ground pork

¼ cup walnut pieces, roughly chopped

2-inch piece fresh ginger, peeled and coarsely grated

1 teaspoon black peppercorns, roughly crushed

1 lb. ready-made puff pastry, thawed if frozen

beaten egg, to glaze

1 teaspoon harissa paste

salt

1. In a large bowl, mix together the pork, walnuts, ginger, pepper, and a little salt.

2. Roll the dough out thinly on a lightly floured surface and trim to a 12-inch square. Cut the square into three strips, 4 inches wide, then brush lightly with beaten egg. Spread a third of the harissa down the center of each, then top with a third of the pork mixture in a narrow log shape.

3. Fold the long edge of the pastry over the filling, and press the edges together with the flattened tip of a small, sharp knife. Trim to neaten if needed, then lightly slash the top of the pastry.

4. Brush with beaten egg, then cut each log into ten pieces and arrange on two lightly oiled cookie sheets. Bake at 400°F for about 20 minutes until golden. Transfer to a wire rack and leave to cool for 20 minutes. Serve warm or cold.

# Perfect Picnic Parcels

With flavors that evoke sunshine on a Greek island, these feta and spinach pockets can be served straight from the oven or at room temperature and with a simple tomato and red onion salad or with a dollop of tzatziki.

———————————

*E*verything seems perfect about the outing to Box Hill in Emma—the weather, the countryside, the guests . . . Seemingly most perfect at all, of course, is Emma herself, as the host of the picnic, Mr. Weston, gallantly points out in his famous conundrum offered over the picnic cloth:

*"What two letters of the alphabet are there, that express perfection?"*
*"What two letters!—express perfection! I am sure I do not know."*
*"Ah! you will never guess. You (to Emma), I am certain, will never guess. I will tell you. M. and A. Em-ma. Do you understand?"*

*The conundrum is lame, not to say untruthful, as the more sensible among the party and we the readers are well aware. Emma is far from perfection, and the picnic too has fallen flat. As the narrator herself with typical irony points out, when the party is en route to the beauty spot, "Nothing was wanting but to be happy when they got there."*

*Oddly, in a novel almost obsessed with food, we don't get to hear anything about the food. Perhaps it was perfect, just like these spinach-and-feta phyllo parcels—the ultimate in picnic foods.*

## SERVES 2

PREP + COOKING TIME: **25** MINUTES

8 cups packed baby spinach leaves
1 cup crumbled feta cheese
large pinch of freshly grated nutmeg
2 tablespoons chopped Italian parsley
4 sheets of phyllo pastry
¼ cup olive oil
salt and black pepper

1. Place the spinach in a large saucepan without any extra water, cover, and cook for 2 minutes until wilted. Drain and squeeze out the excess water.

2. Chop the spinach and mix with the feta, nutmeg, and parsley in a bowl. Season with pepper (the feta is salty, so check before adding salt).

3. Place two sheets of phyllo pastry on top of one another and brush lightly with oil. Place half the filling at the end of the sheet, then fold over to make a triangle and continue folding until the filling is enclosed. Brush with oil and repeat.

4. Place the pockets on a cookie sheet and bake at 400°F for 15 minutes until crisp and golden.

# Stuffed Tomatoes

This healthy dish, packed with good-for-you ingredients, makes a lovely summery lunch and is great served with a crisp salad dressed with a lemony vinaigrette. For a more substantial meal, the stuffed tomatoes are a good accompaniment to broiled fish or chicken.

*In a letter to her sister, Cassandra, in October 1813, Austen wrote: "Have you any tomatas?" "Fanny and I regale on them every day . . ." October is at the very end of the British season of this quintessentially summer fruit-cum-vegetable: Austen and her niece must have been making the most of the fresh produce before winter set in and they would have to make do with the tomato ketchups, chutneys, and jellies that were staples of the Georgian larder.*

*While we are now able to regale on fresh tomatoes all year round, this dish is best made in late summer when there's often a glut of fruits, each jam-packed with flavor.*

## SERVES 4

PREP + COOKING TIME: **45** MINUTES

1⅔ cups vegetable stock
1 generous cup quinoa, rinsed
1 tablespoon extra-virgin olive oil
3 cups chopped cremini mushrooms
2 small zucchini, diced
2 scallions, finely chopped
2 tablespoons toasted sunflower seeds
1 cup chopped basil
finely grated zest of 1 lemon
8 small or 4 large tomatoes
⅔ cup sliced mozzarella cheese
salt and black pepper
crisp salad leaves, to serve

1. Pour the vegetable stock into a medium-size saucepan and bring to a boil. Tip the quinoa into the pan, cover, and simmer gently for 12–15 minutes. Remove from the heat and drain off any stock that hasn't been absorbed.

2. Meanwhile, heat the oil in a large skillet over a medium heat. Add the mushrooms and cook, stirring, for 4–5 minutes, then add the zucchini. Cook for an additional 4–5 minutes, then stir in the scallions, sunflower seeds, basil, lemon zest, and cooked quinoa and season well with salt and pepper.

3. Cut the tops off the tomatoes and scoop out the seeds. Spoon the quinoa mixture into the tomatoes, then top each tomato with the sliced mozzarella. Place on a lightly greased baking sheet. Replace the lids, then bake at 400°F for 15–18 minutes until the mozzarella melts.

# Uppercross Mushroom Pies

These deliciously light mouthfuls of pastry are filled with buttery mushrooms and tarragon. Tarragon has an intense aniseed flavor and partners beautifully with mushrooms, but you could use chervil or chives instead.

———————————•———————•———————————

*M*ushrooms do not make an appearance in Jane Austen's oeuvre, though we know they were widely cooked and enjoyed in Georgian times and in the Austen household. However, if we were to associate the mushroom with any of the major novels, it would be with Persuasion. There the heroine, Anne Elliot, only half-reconciled to the loss of the man she has loved in her youth, goes on a family walk through an autumn landscape of "tawny leaves and withered hedges" in which there must have been no shortage of fungi—ceps, field mushrooms, and puffballs among them. Left largely to her own devices, Anne reflects on her fate but draws solace from the nature around her.

*Imagine Anne has taken a wicker basket with her on her walk and returned to Uppercross—her sister Mary's home—her basket brimming with foraged mushrooms. She hands them over to Mrs. Musgrove's cook, who turns them into these little flavor-packed pies.*

## MAKES 16

PREP + COOKING TIME: **25** MINUTES

16 frozen vol-au-vent cases

3½ tablespoons butter

1 small onion, finely chopped

1 garlic clove, chopped

3½ cups thinly sliced mixed
    mushrooms

½ cup mascarpone cheese

2 teaspoons chopped tarragon, plus
    extra to garnish (optional)

salt and black pepper

1. Line a cookie sheet with parchment paper. Arrange the vol-au-vent cases on it and bake at 425°F for 10–12 minutes, or according to the package instructions, until crisp and golden.

2. Meanwhile, melt the butter in a skillet and cook the onion and garlic over a medium heat for 6–7 minutes, stirring occasionally, until softened and golden. Add the mushrooms and fry for an additional 3–4 minutes, until softened.

3. Stir the mascarpone and tarragon into the pan, add a pinch of salt and pepper, then remove from the heat.

4. Spoon the filling into the pastry cases and serve warm, garnished with extra chopped tarragon, if desired.

# Duck, Pear, and Raspberry Salad

Pears and duck go beautifully together in this easy main-meal salad. The walnuts provide plenty of crunch, and raspberries add color and sharpness. The dressing uses pomegranate molasses, which is not essential but is worth seeking out for the sweet-and-sour note it brings to dishes.

———

*The Georgians were very partial to duck, which was a far more popular fowl on the dinner table than the ubiquitous chicken of today. Breeds of farm ducks such as the heavyweight white Aylesbury were kept in the poultry yard—for their meat and down as well as their eggs—and this was supplemented by the smaller ducks shot out in the wild during autumn and winter on waterfowling expeditions— an extremely popular pastime as well as a way of earning a living.*

*Here we serve duck just as the Georgians liked it: with a fruit accompaniment or condiment to cut through the richness.*

## SERVES 4

PREP + COOKING TIME: 25 MINUTES

2 large, lean duck breasts
2 dessert pears, cored and diced
4 oz. mixed leaf and herb salad
¼ cup walnut pieces
handful of raspberries, to garnish

*For the dressing*

2 teaspoons lime juice
2 teaspoons balsamic vinegar
2 teaspoons pomegranate molasses
   (optional)
2 tablespoons extra-virgin olive oil
salt and black pepper

1. Remove any excess fat from the duck breasts and score the surface using a sharp knife. Heat a ridged pan until hot, then add the duck breasts, skin side down, and cook for 8–10 minutes. Turn them over and cook for an additional 5–10 minutes or until cooked to the pinkness desired. Remove from the pan, cover with foil, and leave to rest.

2. Mix together the diced pears and leaf salad in a bowl. Arrange on serving plates and sprinkle with the walnut pieces.

3. Whisk together all the dressing ingredients in a bowl and season to taste. Drizzle over the salad.

4. Slice the duck breasts and arrange on the salad. Sprinkle with the raspberries and serve immediately.

# Pickled Vegetable Salad

Crunchy and satisfying, this colorful salad is a great side to pair with the Veal Pie (page 94) or the Mushroom Burger (page 102). Or make it a meal in itself by topping with cooked chicken or slices of goat cheese and serving with crusty fresh bread.

———————————————

*The Regency table was above all seasonal—one did not expect, or even want, to eat spring asparagus in a snowstorm or rhubarb when the leaves were falling. The only way to enjoy vegetables as well as many other foodstuffs such as meats, mushrooms, and nuts out of season was to preserve them in some way—very often by pickling—then storing them in a cool larder. The process of pickling involved first steeping the food in brine and then boiling it in water with vinegar, salt, herbs, and spices, thereby capturing all the freshness of the produce while adding an exhilarating piquancy. Salads of pickled vegetables rather like the one here were often served as a side dish to accompany roasted or braised meats.*

## SERVES 4

PREP + COOKING TIME: 40 MINUTES, PLUS COOLING

8 small shallots, peeled

1 small cauliflower, broken into small florets

1 red bell pepper, cored, deseeded, and chopped into ¾-inch pieces

4¼ cups water

⅔ cup white wine vinegar

1 cup green beans

3½ cups sugar snap peas

2 cups watercress

olive oil

salt and black pepper

1. Put the water and vinegar into a heavy-based saucepan, bring to a boil, and add the shallots, cauliflower, and bell pepper. Return the liquid to a boil and boil for 2 minutes. Take the saucepan off the heat and leave the vegetables to cool in the liquid.

2. Half-fill a saucepan with water, lightly salt, and bring to a boil. Add the green beans and sugar snap peas and boil for 1 minute. Drain, rinse with cold water, and drain again.

3. When the pickling liquid is cool, strain the vegetables and mix them with the beans, peas, and watercress in a large salad bowl. Dress with olive oil, season to taste with salt and pepper, and serve.

# Mr. Collins's Pea Soup

Quick and easy, this fresh-tasting soup makes the most of the classic combination of pea and mint, adding delicate leeks and a burst of citrussy flavor from the lemon zest. It's equally good as an elegant appetizer or a light meal.

*M*r. *Collins—the sanctimonious parson in* Pride and Prejudice *—is perhaps the Austen character whom readers most love to loathe. His toadying relationship with his patroness, Lady Catherine de Bourgh, and his self-serving pursuit of a marriage partner which ends with his marriage to Elizabeth Bennet's best friend, Charlotte Lucas, make him hard to like, even if he provides much of the book's comedy. He is not entirely without good points, however: Austen shows him to be an enthusiastic gardener—a quality she would have admired—and no doubt his household, too, benefited from his pursuit in the form of fresh produce for the parsonage table.*

*This summery pea soup might be just one of the dishes that reconciled Mrs. Collins to her fate. And, as she observes to Elizabeth, at least the gardening gets him out of the house and gives her something of a respite, away from his foolishness and absurdities.*

## SERVES 4

PREP + COOKING TIME: **35** MINUTES

2 tablespoons olive oil

4 cups washed and thinly sliced leeks

2½ cups fresh or frozen peas

3¾ cups vegetable stock

2 cups loosely packed mint leaves, plus extra to garnish

¾ cup mascarpone cheese

grated zest of 1 small lemon

salt and black pepper

1. Heat the oil in a saucepan, add the leeks, toss in the oil, then cover and fry gently for 10 minutes, stirring occasionally, until softened but not browned. Mix in the peas and cook briefly.

2. Pour the stock into the pan, add a little salt and pepper, then bring to a boil. Cover and simmer gently for 10 minutes. Ladle half the soup into a blender or food processor, add the mint, and blend until smooth. Pour the puree back into the saucepan.

3. Mix the mascarpone with half the lemon zest, reserving the rest for a garnish. Spoon half the mixture into the soup, then reheat, stirring until the mascarpone has melted. Taste and adjust the seasoning if needed. Ladle the soup into bowls, top with spoonfuls of the remaining mascarpone and a sprinkling of the remaining lemon zest. Garnish with extra mint leaves.

# Pemberley Chestnut Soup

Warming on a winter day, this thick soup has a pleasantly earthy flavor from the chestnuts and is wonderful with a chunk of fresh bread. For vegans, omit the crème fraîche.

*C*hestnuts are one of the trees Elizabeth, in the company of her aunt, Mrs. Gardiner, admires during her visit to Pemberley, Mr. Darcy's seat in Derbyshire. Through the windows of its northern aspect is "a most refreshing view of the high woody hills behind the house, and of the beautiful oaks and Spanish chestnuts which were scattered over the intermediate lawn." Spanish, or sweet, chestnuts were largely planted for ornamental reasons, but no doubt their sweet, delicate fruits were not neglected either. Perhaps, after her marriage, whenever Elizabeth Darcy eats chestnut soup in her new home, we might imagine her thinking back to that first visit to Pemberley when her view of her would-be suitor began to change and she reflected that "to be mistress of Pemberley might be something."

## SERVES 4

PREP + COOKING TIME: **35** MINUTES

¼ cup olive oil

40 sage leaves

2 celery sticks, chopped

2 garlic cloves, chopped

1 red chili, deseeded and chopped

1 teaspoon chopped rosemary

14-oz. can chopped tomatoes

1½ cups vacuum-packed chestnuts

14-oz. can garbanzo beans, rinsed and
    drained

1⅔ cups vegetable stock

salt and black pepper

*To serve*

2 tablespoons olive oil

¼ cup crème fraîche, to serve

1. Heat 3 tablespoons olive oil in a large saucepan until a sage leaf sizzles and crisps in 15–20 seconds, then fry the remaining leaves in batches until crisp, lifting out with a slotted spoon onto a plate lined with paper towels. Set aside.

2. Heat the remaining oil in a saucepan and sauté the celery, garlic, chili, and rosemary for 2–3 minutes.

3. Stir in the tomatoes, chestnuts, and garbanzo beans with the stock and simmer for 8–10 minutes.

4. Remove a third of the soup and blend, using a hand blender or in a food processor or blender, to give a thick consistency. Return to the pan, season, and serve with a swirl of olive oil, a dollop of crème fraîche, and a few crispy sage leaves.

# Mary Musgrove's Meat Platter

Sweet juicy figs contrast beautifully with the salty prosciutto in this elegantly simple meat platter. You could replace the figs and prosciutto with ham and the Peach Pickle (page 61) or beef with the Plum and Crushed Peppercorn Jelly (page 58).

---

*W*hile luncheon was not quite the ladylike meal it would later become—being the preserve of laborers and working gentlemen who needed something to sustain them through the middle of the day—this does not mean that the women of Austen's class did not occasionally treat themselves to a light—or not-so-light—bite in the early afternoon. In Persuasion, Mary Musgrove, Anne Elliot's indolent, self-entitled sister, is persuaded to rise from her favorite spot—the "faded sofa of the pretty little drawing-room" in her home at Uppercross—to eat a little meat and finally go for a walk up to the Great House, the home of her in-laws.

## SERVES 4

PREP TIME: 15 MINUTES

8 figs

4 oz. mozzarella cheese, cut into 8 slices

8 slices of prosciutto

7 tablespoons extra-virgin olive oil

2 tablespoons balsamic vinegar

2 cups arugula leaves

salt and black pepper

1. Cut a deep cross into the top of each fig, nearly to the bottom, then place a piece of mozzarella inside. Wrap a slice of prosciutto around each fig. Brush the prosciutto with a little oil. Transfer to a cookie sheet and bake at 425°F for 7–10 minutes or until the ham is crisp and the cheese starts to melt.

2. Meanwhile, whisk together the balsamic vinegar with the remaining oil and season well. Toss most of the dressing together with the arugula leaves and arrange on plates. Add the figs and drizzle with a little more of the dressing. Serve immediately.

# Dr. Grant's Sandwich Tray

It's hard to beat a sandwich for convenience—neatly portable for lunch or a snack on the go—and versatility. There's a huge array of possible fillings, and these recipes showcase three especially good ones: turkey and cranberry with peppery watercress, mouthwatering fried steak with caramelized leeks, and a classic club sandwich.

*We all know the story about the "invention" of the sandwich by the politician John Montagu, 4th Earl of Sandwich (1718–92), who, when he wanted a bite to eat during a particularly protracted card game, ordered a snack of "a bit of beef, between two slices of toasted bread" that he could consume without leaving the table. No doubt the earl helped popularize the sandwich, but there is quite a lot of evidence to suggest that the notion had been around for some time before. It is hardly an act of culinary genius.*

*Whatever its origins, by Jane Austen's time sandwiches were a popular light refreshment served to guests, as we see is the case at Dr. Grant's rectory in Mansfield Park, where the hero, Edmund Bertram, goes visiting, ready to fall in love with the rector's niece, Mary Crawford:*

> *A young woman, pretty, lively, with a harp as elegant as herself, and both placed near a window, cut down to the ground, and opening on a little lawn, surrounded by shrubs in the rich foliage of summer, was enough to catch any man's heart. The season, the scene, the air, were all favourable to tenderness and sentiment. Mrs. Grant and her tambour frame were not without their use: it was all in harmony; and as everything will turn to account when love is once set going, even the sandwich tray, and Dr. Grant doing the honours of it, were worth looking at.*

*We would like to think that the following sandwiches are good for eating as well as looking at . . . and perhaps for falling in love over, too.*

# Turkey, Watercress, Cranberry Sauce, and Mayo

MAKES 4

PREP TIME: 10 MINUTES

8 slices of white bread
3 tablespoons cranberry sauce
1 cup watercress
4–8 slices cooked turkey
1 large avocado, peeled, pitted, and sliced
3 tablespoons mayonnaise

1. Spread four slices of the bread with the cranberry sauce.

2. Divide the watercress between the slices of bread, then top with the turkey slices, followed by the sliced avocado.

3. Spread the remaining slices of bread with the mayonnaise and place on top to make four sandwiches.

# Beef Steak and Caramelized Leek

MAKES 4

PREP + COOKING TIME: 20 MINUTES

2 tablespoons butter
1 tablespoon olive oil
2 leeks, trimmed and sliced
1 tablespoon brown sugar
1 tablespoon white wine
4 sirloin steaks, about 5 oz. each
2 teaspoons horseradish sauce
2 tablespoons mayonnaise
4 ciabatta rolls

1. Heat the butter and olive oil in a skillet, add the leeks, and cook over a low heat for 10 minutes, stirring occasionally. Add the brown sugar and white wine and cook for an additional 5 minutes.

2. Meanwhile, heat a grill pan until hot, add the steaks, and cook for 3–4 minutes on each side, or until cooked to your liking. Leave to rest.

3. Mix the horseradish and mayonnaise in a small bowl.

4. Halve and toast the ciabatta rolls, then spread the bases with the horseradish mayonnaise. Top each base with a steak and the caramelized leeks, then add the lids and serve.

# Club Sandwich

A great way to use up leftover cooked chicken, plus creamy avocado, juicy tomatoes, and crisp bacon, this sandwich is a winning combination of flavors and textures. You can also pep it up by adding a little thinly sliced red onion.

## SERVES 4

PREP + COOKING TIME: **20** MINUTES

4 slices of Canadian bacon

8 slices of whole-wheat bread

2 teaspoons Dijon mustard

4 crisp iceberg lettuce leaves

4 tomatoes, sliced

2 cooked chicken breasts, sliced

1 avocado, pitted, peeled, and sliced

1. Fry the bacon slices in a dry skillet until crisp.

2. Meanwhile, toast the bread on both sides, then spread four slices with the mustard.

3. Place a lettuce leaf on each of these slices and top with the sliced tomato. Divide the chicken between the slices of toast.

4. Top with the bacon and the avocado.

5. Finish with the remaining slices of toast and, using toothpicks to keep the sandwiches together, cut on the diagonal to serve.

# Plum and Crushed Peppercorn Jelly

This unusual sweet and spicy jelly works well served with roast lamb and roast potatoes, and makes a humble cheese sandwich something special. It's also great dolloped on cold cream cheese spread on a cracker. Once opened, it should be stored in the refrigerator.

———————

*This savory jelly makes the most out of the tongue-tingling warmth of crushed peppercorns—a spice that the Georgians, through the eighteenth century, had learned to love again. From ancient times, the peppercorn trade out of South Asia had been a valuable one, so much so that it earned the nickname "black gold." A luxury in the kitchens of medieval Europe, it fell out of favor in the Renaissance, when it was thought to cause melancholy and there was a preference for other spices such as nutmeg and cloves. In the eighteenth century the ascendance of French cuisine, in which salt and pepper were paired as the essential seasoning, soon influenced tastes across the Channel—and it has not left the British kitchen since.*

## MAKES 7 JARS

PREP + COOKING TIME: 1 HOUR, PLUS STRAINING

4 lb. plums

5 cups water

about 6 cups sugar

2 teaspoons multicolored peppercorns, roughly crushed

2 teaspoons pink peppercorns, either dried or in brine, roughly crushed

1 tablespoon butter (optional)

1. Add the plums and measured water to the preserving pan (there's no need to pit or slice the plums first). Bring to a boil, then cover, and cook gently for 30 minutes, stirring and mashing the fruit from time to time with a fork, until soft.

2. Allow to cool slightly, then pour into a scalded jelly bag suspended over a large bowl and allow to drip for several hours.

3. Measure the clear liquid and pour back into the rinsed preserving pan. Weigh 1 lb. sugar for every 2½ cups of liquid, then pour into the preserving pan. Add the peppercorns and heat gently, stirring from time to time, until the sugar has dissolved.

4. Bring to a boil, then boil rapidly until setting point is reached (10–20 minutes). Skim with a slotted spoon or stir in the butter to reduce foaming. Allow to stand for 5 minutes so that the peppercorns don't float to the surface.

5. Ladle into warm, dry jars, filling to the very top. Screw on the lids, label, and leave to cool.

# Chestnut Jelly with Whiskey

This sweet and earthy chestnut jelly is perfect for spooning over yogurt or a good chunk of crusty bread. While using authentic Scotch whiskey is recommended, whichever whiskey you have available will do the job.

---

*Elopement—usually to Scotland's Gretna Green, where the marriage laws were much looser—was something of a commonplace in Georgian literature: it is the most dastardly thing an upper-class man can do to a woman, threatening not only her reputation but that of the entire family who has allowed such a thing to happen. In Jane Austen, there are elopements or planned elopements in* Pride and Prejudice *(George Wickham with Georgiana Darcy and, subsequently, Lydia Bennet) and* Mansfield Park *(John Yates and Julia Bertram), while, in* Sense and Sensibility, *the melancholic, Byronic hero Colonel Brandon has in his youth attempted to elope with his cousin Eliza, though here the episode is given a more romantic tinge.*

*Here's a recipe that a Gretna Green landlady might have served to any of Austen's eloping couples—a delicious whiskey-flavored chestnut jelly—though, of course, it's more than any of them deserve!*

## MAKES 2 JARS

PREP + COOKING TIME: **1** HOUR

1 lb. cooked, peeled chestnuts
1 vanilla pod
1½ cups soft light brown sugar
2 tablespoons whiskey

1. Put the chestnuts and vanilla pod into a heavy-based pan and add enough water to just cover them. Bring to a boil, then reduce the heat, cover the pan, and simmer for 30 minutes. Remove the vanilla pod and set aside, then strain and reserve the cooking liquid. Puree the chestnuts in a food processor or blender, adding a little of the reserved liquid if necessary.

2. Put the puree back into the pan. Slice the vanilla pod lengthwise and scrape the seeds into the pan.

3. Add the sugar and 3 fl. oz. of the cooking liquid and stir to blend. Bring to a boil, stirring frequently, and cook for about 5 minutes, or until very thick. Remove from the heat and add the whiskey.

4. Ladle into warm, dry jars. Cover with screw-top lids, or with wax-paper discs and cellophane tops secured with elastic bands. Label and leave to mature for two days in a cool, dark place.

5. To serve, layer spoonfuls of jelly in small glasses with honey-flavored yogurt.

# Mrs. Reynolds's Peach Pickle

When ripe peaches are plentiful and cheap in summer, pickle some to enjoy in winter. These peaches go well with slices of ham, roast pork or duck, and blue cheese. The recipe works well with nectarines also.

———————————————

*T*he next variation which their visit afforded was produced by the entrance of servants with cold meat, cake, and a variety of all the finest fruits in season; but this did not take place till after many a significant look and smile from Mrs. Annesley (Miss Darcy's companion) to Miss Darcy had been given, to remind her of her post. There was now employment for the whole party—for though they could not all talk, they could all eat; and the beautiful pyramids of grapes, nectarines, and peaches soon collected them round the table.

The appearance of peaches, along with grapes and nectarines, in the drawing room at Pemberley, when Elizabeth and her aunt call on Miss Darcy, signals to both the heroine and to us, the readers, the absolute state of luxury in which the Darcys live. The growing of such fruits required the building and maintenance of costly hothouses, which were kept sultry by braziers or furnaces and, after 1818, by hot water piped into the building.

Fresh peaches should always be a luxury—enjoyed for that brief season at the height of summer. That said, something of the fragrance and sweetness of a good peach can be enjoyed all year round, in the form of our Mrs. Reynolds's Peach Pickle— named in honor of Fitzwilliam and Georgiana Darcy's housekeeper, who, we infer, has largely brought them up.

Continued ⇀

## MAKES 1 LARGE JAR

PREP + COOKING TIME: 35 MINUTES

1¼ cups white malt vinegar

5 cups sugar

1 teaspoon whole cloves

1 teaspoon whole allspice berries

3-inch piece cinnamon stick, halved

2 lb. small peaches, halved and pitted

1. Pour the vinegar into a large saucepan, add the sugar and spices, and heat gently until the sugar has dissolved. Add the peach halves and cook very gently for 4–5 minutes until just tender but still firm. Lift out of the syrup with a slotted spoon and pack tightly into a warmed large jar.

2. Boil the syrup for 2–3 minutes to concentrate the flavors, then pour over the fruit, making sure that the fruit is completely covered and the jar filled to the very top. Top up with a little extra warm vinegar if needed.

3. Add a small piece of crumpled wax paper to stop the fruit from rising out of the vinegar in the jar. Screw or clip on the lid, label, and leave to cool.

4. After a few hours, the peaches will begin to rise in the jar, but as they become saturated with the syrup they will sink once more; at this point they will be ready to eat.

# Captain Frederick Wentworth's Ship's Biscuits

These seeded oat crackers are the perfect vehicle for all kinds of toppings, from cheese and smoked salmon to nut butter or hummus. Stored in an airtight container, they will keep for up to a week.

*From the seventeenth to the late nineteenth century, the sailor's "bread" was hard biscuits—later known as hardtack—made of nothing but wheat flour and water, with no salt to add flavor or yeast to leaven. Even the wheat flour used was of a cheap, coarse kind, and the less honest of the victuallers who supplied the navy sometimes got away with substituting even cheaper flours made from rye, barley, or horse beans. Ship's biscuits must have been unappetizing if filling (each man in the Royal Navy was entitled to a pound of biscuits a day), and the sailors must really have longed for those times anchored in port when they had access to good fresh bread.*

*The sailors were also entitled to a ration of oatmeal every week—used for making gruel—so here we have imagined a new, improved kind of ship's biscuit made with oats, perhaps dispensed by that most benevolent of Royal Navy captains, Frederick Wentworth. Wonderful accompanied by those other maritime staples, cheese and beer.*

## MAKES 20

PREP + COOKING TIME: **40** MINUTES

1 cup oatmeal

generous ½ cup all-purpose flour, plus extra for dusting

¼ cup mixed seeds, such as poppy seeds, flaxseeds, and sesame seeds

½ teaspoon celery salt or sea salt

½ teaspoon black pepper

3½ tablespoons butter, chilled and diced

5 tablespoons cold water

1. Put the oatmeal, flour, seeds, salt, and pepper in a bowl or food processor. Add the butter and rub in with your fingertips or process until the mixture resembles bread crumbs. Add the measured water and mix or blend to a firm dough, adding a little more water if the dough feels dry.

2. Roll out the dough on a lightly floured surface to ⅛ inch thick. Cut out 20 rounds using a 2½-inch plain or fluted cookie cutter, rerolling the trimmings to make more. Place slightly apart on a large greased cookie sheet.

3. Bake at 350°F for about 25 minutes until firm. Transfer to a wire rack to cool.

# Georgian Fruit Salad

The rosewater syrup in this fruit salad gives it an enticing scent. Delicious on its own or with thick yogurt for breakfast or served with vanilla ice cream for dessert, you can use this recipe as a template and add whatever you have in the fruit bowl or refrigerator. Spring and summer fruits work especially well with the floral scent of rosewater here.

———————————————•———————————————

*The Georgians were extremely fond of using rosewater—and indeed other floral distillates such as orange flower water—in their desserts, custards, creams, cakes, and biscuits, though seldom in their savory dishes. This fragrant fruit salad will take you straight back to Regency England and to the dessert course of a leisurely dinner in one of "Austen's houses." It's up to you to take your pick—whether it's the fashionable formality of Netherfield Park, Mr. Bingley's rented home in* Pride and Prejudice, *or the cozier affair of the Dashwoods' cottage in Devon in* Sense and Sensibility.

## SERVES 4

PREP + COOKING TIME: 15 MINUTES

2 tablespoons rosewater

2 tablespoons honey

juice of ½ lemon

¼ watermelon

½ galia melon

1 mango

2 green apples

2 bananas

3 kiwifruit

1 cup strawberries

1 cup blueberries

1. Mix the rosewater, honey, and lemon juice together until combined.

2. Peel and deseed both the melons and cut the flesh into 1-inch chunks. Put them in a large bowl.

3. Peel and dice the mango, dice the apples, and slice the bananas. Add to the bowl with the melon.

4. Peel the kiwifruit and cut the flesh into rounds, add to the bowl along with the berries, and mix the fruit together carefully.

5. Drizzle with the rosewater syrup. Stir gently to coat and spoon into serving bowls.

# Strawberry and Lavender Shortcakes

Lavender and strawberries: the scents and tastes of summer are combined in edible form in these delectable shortcakes. They are best eaten on the day they are filled, but the plain cookies can be stored in an airtight container for up to three days.

N*o Georgian household was without a good store of lavender water. This was often made at home by gently simmering fresh or dried lavender buds in water and then pouring the resulting essence through a sieve or a cheesecloth. Alternatively and more simply, as recommended by Martha Lloyd, Jane Austen's close friend, it could be made by mixing store-bought lavender oil, alcohol, and a little ambergris.*

*Lavender water was often sprinkled on laundry, especially bed linen and undergarments, to help keep them fresh and fragrant; it was used as a cosmetic for skin and hair and to cover up food smells in the kitchen; and it was also dispensed as a home remedy to treat rashes, cuts, and sunburn. We see its last use in action in* Sense and Sensibility, *where the three-year-old daughter of Lady Middleton receives a scratch on her neck from a pin and is at once ministered to by being "covered with kisses" and having "her wound bathed with lavender-water . . . and her mouth stuffed with sugar plums."*

*Lavender must have been one of the pervasive smells of the Regency household. While rarely used in Georgian cooking—perhaps indeed because of its very ubiquity in other areas of household life—our shortcakes here gently evoke its deep floral essence.*

Continued ⇥

## MAKES 8

PREP + COOKING TIME: 45 MINUTES

1¼ cups all-purpose flour
¼ cup ground rice
9 tablespoons butter, diced
4 tablespoons superfine sugar
1 tablespoon lavender petals

*To decorate*

2 cups strawberries
⅔ cup heavy cream
16 small lavender flowers (optional)
sifted confectioners' sugar, for dusting

1. Put the flour and ground rice in a mixing bowl or a food processor. Add the butter and rub in with your fingertips or process until the mixture resembles fine bread crumbs.

2. Stir in the sugar and lavender petals and squeeze the crumbs together with your hands to form a smooth ball. Knead lightly, then roll out on a lightly floured surface until ¼ inch thick. Cut out 3-inch circles using a fluted round cookie cutter. Transfer to an ungreased cookie sheet. Knead the trimmings and continue rolling and stamping out until you have made 16 cookies.

3. Prick with a fork, then bake at 325°F for 10–12 minutes until pale golden. Leave to cool on the cookie sheet.

4. To serve, halve four of the smallest strawberries; hull and slice the rest. Whip the cream and spoon over eight of the cookies. Top with the sliced strawberries and then the remaining cookies. Spoon the remaining cream on top and decorate with the reserved halved strawberries and tiny sprigs of lavender, if desired. Dust lightly with sifted confectioners' sugar.

# Mrs. Morland's Gingered Pear Juice

Put a zip in your step with this sweet pear juice that has a kick of spice from the ginger. And it's good for you, too—the pear will provide fiber and vitamins, while ginger is loaded with antioxidants.

*B*lessed *with a large and lively extended family of her own, with plenty of nephews and nieces of whom she was more or less fond, it is unsurprising that Jane Austen excelled at portraying young families, their infuriating faults as well as their charms. One of her freshest portraits of such a family is the Morlands in Northanger Abbey.*

*With no fewer than ten children, Mrs. Morland, the wife of a comfortable country clergyman, has her work cut out for her, especially as far as her tomboy of an eldest daughter, Catherine—the novel's heroine—is concerned—averse to lessons and "greatly preferring cricket not merely to dolls, but to the more heroic enjoyments of infancy, nursing a dormouse, feeding a canary-bird, or watering a rose-bush." There must have been some quieter moments in the rough and tumble of the Morland parsonage, though, and perhaps in late summer when the children had exhausted themselves playing, Mrs. Morland brought them in for a glass of her famous gingered pear juice, made from fruit from the parsonage orchard.*

## SERVES 1

PREP TIME: 5 MINUTES

¾-inch piece fresh ginger, peeled
5 pears, roughly chopped
large pinch of ground cinnamon
ice cubes

1. Add the ginger and pears to a juicer and juice, then stir in the cinnamon.

2. Pour the juice into a glass over ice cubes and serve immediately.

# William Cowper's Poetical Melon Cooler

Heaven on a hot day, this refreshing fruity cooler is a breeze to make—a bit of chopping, freezing, and blending is all it takes. You can ring the changes by using rock melon instead of watermelon.

---

*B*y the eighteenth century, gardening had established itself as a genteel pursuit and a subject of scientific study. Gentlemen gardeners concerned themselves particularly with the growing of fruits and vegetables, especially those not native to Great Britain that required particular scientific care, and the use of technologies such as hothouses. Here is William Cowper (1731–1800)—perhaps Jane Austen's favorite poet, whom she mentions often in her letters—writing on his growing passion for gardening in 1788:

> I then judged it high time to exchange this occupation [translating Homer] for another . . . gardening was, of all employments, that in which I succeeded best, though even in this I didn't suddenly attain perfection. I began with lettuces and cauliflowers; from then I proceeded to cucumbers; next to melons.

Being extremely difficult, melon growing—especially out of season—represented one of the pinnacles of the gardener's skill, an art and science all in one. Jane Austen's own garden at Chawton was far too modest for growing such a fruit, though we might well imagine that her brother Edward grew them at Chawton House.

Here's a refreshing drink for a summer day—perhaps prepared for Mr. Cowper as he tended to his melon beds and composed his nature poems in his head.

## SERVES 2

PREP TIME: 10 MINUTES, PLUS FREEZING

1 cup diced and deseeded watermelon
1 cup strawberries, hulled
½ cup water
small handful of mint or tarragon leaves, plus extra to decorate (optional)

1. Freeze the melon and strawberries until solid.

2. Put the frozen melon and strawberries in a food processor or blender, add the water and the mint or tarragon, and process until smooth.

3. Pour the mixture into two short glasses, decorate with mint or tarragon leaves, if desired, and serve immediately.

# Picnicking Regency Style

Picnics today are usually informal affairs. Perhaps we stuff a packet of sandwiches, some fruit, and a vacuum flask of tea into our backpack; we stop willy-nilly while out on our walk, sitting on a tree stump or a rocky outcrop, if we're lucky; and, having packed the wrappers or orange peel back into our backpack, continue on our way after a scant half-hour or so. If we or our parents ever had a picnic basket and blanket, they are stowed away in an attic or basement, long forgotten.

The Regency picnic was, by contrast, formal and highly organized, involving at least as much preparation as any grand dinner. The site was carefully chosen—perhaps under the shade of an ancient oak and preferably with a picturesque view; the food was lavish and plentiful; and there was furniture—if not actual chairs and stools and a table, then at least a large rug and cushions. All this involved a lot of labor—with manservants required to carry the picnic baskets up to the chosen site; lay out the dishes, plates, and silverware; and then clear it all away again. The Regency picnic was both preposterous and wonderful—one modern commentator has even called it a way of "performing Britishness," an expression of national identity.

The late Georgian picnicking craze was just one facet of the phenomenon known as Romanticism. Other facets included the nature poetry of figures like William Wordsworth (1770–1850), whose famous "I Wandered Lonely as a Cloud" was published in 1807; the stirring landscape art of J. M. W. Turner (1775–1851) as well as the popularity of amateur watercolor painting; the cult of the picturesque view and scenic touring; the fashions for country walking and even for open-air swimming (we might think of Lord Byron's feat of swimming across the Hellespont in 1810); and a new fascination with the sea and the seaside. As the Industrial Revolution got under way, with all its dirt and ugliness and "dark Satanic mills" (William Blake, 1804), the elite turned, quite literally, toward Nature, with a capital N—to "England's green & pleasant Land" (Blake again, of course).

We find many of these Romantic pastimes and tropes in Jane Austen's novels, though they are often gently mocked or shown to be problematic if taken too seriously. Marianne Dashwood's Romantic walks lead her to a fall and a sprained ankle and, eventually, to a broken heart; the stroll to view the sea in Lyme in Persuasion ends in disaster when Louisa Musgrove falls from the Cobb; in Sanditon, seaside bathing is exposed as not much more than a moneymaking venture designed to exploit people's health worries. And so, too, in Emma, a picnic that appears superficially idyllic ends up exposing the underlying tensions and disconnections between the characters.

The outing to Box Hill is perhaps the most famous picnic in literature (along with the even more fateful picnic at Hanging Rock)—just as Èdouard Manet's Le Déjeuner sur l'herbe (1862–63) is the most famous picnic in art (though there's no nudity in Emma!). As ever in Jane Austen, anything that stifles natural human relations beneath too strict formality and convention, whether that be the overcrowded Assembly Rooms at Bath or a stuffy dinner or even a scenic picnic, is bound to lead to trouble. At the Box Hill picnic, for all the participants' expectation of pleasure, disharmony reigns and this leads to what is perhaps one of the most painful moments in all of literature—when Emma, in an attempt to enliven the proceedings, makes cruel fun of Miss Bates, wounding that vulnerable, voluble woman deeply. At least the picnic provides the hidden turning point of the novel, as the heroine begins to become belatedly aware of her wider human responsibilities.

# Dinner

*D*inner was something of a "movable feast," its exact timing depending on one's class, where one lived, one's occupation, and even the time of year. In the first half of the eighteenth century, everyone had eaten dinner early—perhaps as early as eleven o'clock—but as the decades passed the meal took place later and later, at least among the aristocratic and gentry classes.

By the Regency period proper, fashionable city dwellers might sit down to dine as late as eight o'clock, although in the countryside the landed gentry dined around four or four-thirty, to catch the remaining daylight. In Pride and Prejudice, only at the luxurious Netherfield, the temporary home of Mr. Bingley, is dinner eaten fashionably later. This required candles, a notable expense in any household.

The typical dinner table of the well-to-do would be spread with a large number of dishes, both savory and sweet—encompassing soups, roast meats (especially beef, game, and venison), pies, and syllabubs. Sometimes, at the end of one such "course," servants would set a fresh cloth for another, before the meal came to a close with a dessert course of ices, fruits, and other elaborate puddings. The appetite of the Georgians at table seems stupendous to modern eyes—leaving us both to wonder at the slender silhouette of Empire gowns and to be not surprised at all by the bulging girth of the Prince Regent, unkindly described by one contemporary as a "great sausage stuffed into the covering." In the following recipes, we have slimmed things down somewhat, evoking the style with less of the "substance."

# Netherfield White Soup

Eggs, Parmesan, and soft bread crumbs are whisked into this simple soup to make it smooth, creamy, and delicious. Ready in under 15 minutes, it's a recipe you'll turn to time and again. Use good-quality chicken stock, preferably homemade, for the best results.

*W*hite soup was clearly quite a thing at a ball of any pretension in Georgian times. When, in Pride and Prejudice, Mr. Bingley's snobbish sister Caroline asks whether he really is going to go ahead with his plan to hold a dance at Netherfield (which "for some of us," she says, would be "a punishment [rather] than a pleasure"), he tells her that it is "quite a settled thing . . . as soon as Nicholls has made white soup enough I shall send round my cards."

*We may well wonder at the soup being made quite so early—but preparations for the sit-down supper at the ball would have made the Netherfield kitchens a very busy place for a more than a few days before the great evening itself. Regency white soup called for veal stock and copious amounts of ground almonds—and both of these could have sensibly been made in advance. This modern take, however, is a simpler affair, though it is every bit as delicious.*

## SERVES 4

PREP + COOKING TIME: 12 MINUTES

5 cups chicken stock

4 eggs

⅓ cup grated Parmesan cheese, plus extra to serve

2 tablespoons fresh white bread crumbs

¼ teaspoon grated nutmeg

salt and white pepper

basil leaves, to garnish

1. Put the stock in a saucepan and bring to a boil. Reduce the heat and simmer for 2–3 minutes. Beat the eggs, Parmesan, bread crumbs, and nutmeg in a bowl and season generously. Gradually whisk in two ladlesful of hot stock into the egg mixture.

2. Reduce the heat under the saucepan, then slowly stir the egg mixture into the stock until smooth, making sure the temperature remains moderate, as the egg will curdle if the soup boils. Gently simmer for 2–3 minutes until piping hot.

3. Ladle the soup into bowls, tear the basil leaves into pieces, and sprinkle over the soup. Serve with extra Parmesan.

# Salmagundi

This is a great summer salad when tomatoes are at peak flavor. It's also ideal as a make-ahead dish as the taste improves the longer the vegetable and herb mixture sits, but don't add the flatbreads or tortillas until just before serving, so they stay crunchy.

———————————

*P*opular as a first course through the eighteenth and early nineteenth century, salmagundi, or "cold hash," was always more of a concept than a recipe—the salade composée of its day. As Hannah Glasse—who gives three recipes for the salad in her* The Art of Cookery Made Plain and Easy *(1747)—points out: "You may always make a Salamongundy of such things as you have, according to your fancy."*

*Typical ingredients might include everything from roast meats and seafood to salad leaves, nuts, and herbs, with the finished arrangement often strewn with flowers such as nasturtiums or violets. There was always a dressing of some kind. What mattered, however, was that salmagundi should be as colorful, varied in texture, and tasty as could be.*

## SERVES 4–6

PREP + COOKING TIME: 15 MINUTES, PLUS COOLING

2 whole-wheat flatbreads
1 large green bell pepper, cored, deseeded, and diced
1 cucumber, diced
1¾ cups cherry tomatoes, halved
½ red onion, finely chopped
2 tablespoons chopped mint
2 tablespoons chopped Italian parsley
2 tablespoons chopped cilantro
3 tablespoons olive oil
juice of 1 lemon
salt and black pepper

1. Toast the flatbreads or tortillas on a preheated ridged grill pan or under a preheated hot broiler for 2–3 minutes or until charred. Leave to cool, then tear into bite-size pieces.

2. Put the bell pepper, cucumber, tomatoes, onion, and herbs in a serving bowl, add the oil and lemon juice, and season with salt and pepper, tossing well. Add the bread and stir again. Serve immediately.

# Lyme Bay Mackerel

Packed with health-boosting vegetables along with omega-3-rich mackerel, this is a great summer meal. For something slightly heartier, try bulgur wheat or brown rice in place of the couscous.

————————————

*U*ndoubtedly the most famous and dramatic scene in Persuasion *takes place in the fashionable resort of Lyme Regis, on the Dorset coast: during a stroll along the town's picturesque harbor wall, known as the Cobb, Louisa Musgrove foolishly attempts to jump off the upper walkway onto the lower and receives a severe concussion. It is Anne Elliot's good sense during the crisis that provides the turning point in the narrative and the heroine's life, as Captain Wentworth begins to reassess the woman who rejected him seven years before. As all the party look to Anne to sort out the situation, "Captain Wentworth's eyes," Austen tells us, "were also turned towards her." It is as if he sees her for the first time since their reacquaintance.*

*Lyme Bay and the Dorset coast have a long tradition of mackerel fishing, so we might well imagine our fashionable party—as the end of their stressful, fateful day—settling down in their lodgings to a heartening meal of freshly caught fish.*

## SERVES 4

PREP + COOKING TIME: **25** MINUTES

1 cup couscous

1 cup green beans, halved

¾ cup fresh or frozen peas

1 cup asparagus tips

4 scallions, sliced

2 garlic cloves, finely diced

¼ cup chopped mint

¼ cup chopped Italian parsley

3 peppered smoked mackerel fillets,
  skinned and flaked

3 tablespoons olive oil

juice of 1 lime

1 romaine lettuce, roughly torn

12 cherry tomatoes, halved

2 tablespoons toasted pine nuts

salt and black pepper

1. Place the couscous in a large, heatproof bowl and just cover with boiling water. Leave to stand for 15 minutes.

2. Meanwhile, steam or boil the green beans, peas, and asparagus tips for 4–5 minutes until just tender. Rinse under cold running water and drain.

3. Fluff up the couscous with a fork, then stir in the spring onions, garlic, herbs, mackerel, oil, and lime juice. Season to taste.

4. Arrange the lettuce and tomatoes on a serving plate, spoon over the couscous, and sprinkle with the pine nuts.

# Cassandra's Lobster and Asparagus

This is the recipe to have up your sleeve when you want to impress: lobster tails with a creamy, cheesy filling alongside buttery asparagus is a combination that all your guests will be sure to love.

*I* *n one of the many affectionate letters Austen wrote to her sister Cassandra, Austen describes how a dinner at an inn of "asparagus and a lobster . . . made me wish for you." Why this particular dish reminded her so much of her sister is not entirely clear—though perhaps it was simply because it was one of Cassandra's favorites. However, what it does bear witness to, most importantly, is the role food played in their intimacy. Since childhood they would have tended the kitchen garden together, looked after the poultry yard together, no doubt cooked and baked a little together, and, above all, dined together—sharing the pleasures of eating and talking at the family table.*

## SERVES 4

PREP + COOKING TIME: 25 MINUTES

¼ cup butter
1 tablespoon olive oil
1 shallot, finely chopped
3 tablespoons dry sherry
1 teaspoon Dijon mustard
scant ½ cup sour cream
2 small ready-cooked lobsters, about
   1 lb. 5 oz. each
½ cup shredded Gruyère cheese
1 lb. asparagus spears, trimmed
salt and black pepper

1. Heat half the butter and oil in a small saucepan. Add the shallot and cook for 5 minutes until softened. Pour over the sherry and cook for 2 minutes until nearly boiled away. Stir in the mustard and sour cream, heat through, and season with salt.

2. Meanwhile, using a large knife, cut the lobsters in half lengthwise. Remove the meat from the tail and claws, reserving the main shell halves. Cut the lobster meat into large chunks.

3. Add the lobster meat to the sauce and warm through. Carefully spoon into the tail cavities of the reserved lobster shell halves and sprinkle with the Gruyère. Cook under a preheated hot broiler for 3–5 minutes until golden and bubbling.

4. Meanwhile, place the asparagus in a skillet over a medium heat and add just enough water to cover the base of the skillet. Put the lid on and let the asparagus steam for 3–5 minutes, until tender. Add the remaining butter and toss the asparagus in the butter as it melts.

5. Season with salt and pepper and serve with the lobster.

# Mr. Gardiner's Slow-Cooked Fish

A good choice for when you are entertaining—all the prep can be done ahead with this slow cooker recipe, and all you need do at the last minute is make a salad and steam some tiny new potatoes to serve with it.

———————————————•———————————————

*A*long with game shooting, angling was another popular gentlemanly pursuit of Jane Austen's time. Like game, freshwater fish such as trout, bream, and pike would have quite often appeared on the tables of Regency country houses. The keenest angler in Jane Austen's fiction is undoubtedly Elizabeth Bennet's amiable uncle, Mr. Gardiner who, during their visit to Pemberley, admires Mr. Darcy's trout stream:

> Mr. Gardiner, though seldom able to indulge the taste, was very fond of fishing, and was so much engaged in watching the occasional appearance of some trout in the water . . . that he advanced but little . . . The conversation soon turned upon fishing, and she [Elizabeth] heard Mr. Darcy invite him, with the greatest civility, to fish there as often as he chose while he continued in the neighbourhood, offering at the same time to supply him with fishing tackle, and pointing out those parts of the stream where there was usually most sport.

## SERVES 4

PREP + COOKING TIME: 2 HOURS

3½ tablespoons butter, at room temperature
grated zest and juice of 1 lemon
4 trout fillets, skinned
1 flounder, filleted into 4 pieces, skinned
scant 1 cup boiling fish stock
3 egg yolks
salt and black pepper

1. Preheat the slow cooker. Beat the butter with the lemon zest and a little salt and pepper.

2. Lay the trout fillets on a chopping board, skinned sides uppermost. Trim the edges to neaten, if needed, and spread with half the lemon butter. Top with the flounder fillets, skinned side uppermost, and spread with the remaining butter. Roll up each fish stack, starting at the tapered end. Secure each spiral with two toothpicks at right angles to each other and arrange in the base of the slow cooker pot.

3. Pour the lemon juice and boiling stock over the fish and add a little salt and pepper. Cover with the lid and cook on low for 1½–2 hours or until the fish flakes easily when pressed in the center with a knife.

4. Lift out the fish with a slotted spoon, put onto a serving plate, and remove the toothpicks. Strain the cooking juices into a bowl. Put the egg yolks in a saucepan and gradually whisk in the strained stock until smooth. Cook over a medium heat, whisking constantly without boiling, for 3–4 minutes or until lightly thickened and foamy. Serve the fish with a generous drizzle of the sauce around each one.

# Mansfield Wood Roast Pheasant

The meat in this sensational roast is enhanced by punchy woodland flavors from the dried mushrooms and fresh thyme, while the red currant jelly brings a note of sweetness. Serve with steamed cabbage or spinach and with creamy mashed potatoes to mop up the wonderful gravy.

---

*After Sir Thomas Bertram's unexpected return from Antigua to Mansfield Park, to discover both his house and family in all kinds of disarray, his oldest son, Tom, attempts to distract him with talk about the estate's pheasant shoots. It is October, just after the beginning of the pheasant season, and there has been some good shooting for him and his brother, Edmund:*

> *We brought home six brace between us, and might each have killed six times as many; but we respect your pheasants, sir, I assure you, as much as you could desire. I do not think you will find your woods by any means worse stocked than they were. I never saw Mansfield Wood so full of pheasants in my life as this year.*

*For Britain's country estates, pheasant shooting was an important source of meat for the table, as well as a healthy recreation for young men, like Tom, who might otherwise have little to do with themselves. With "six brace" between them, the brothers had plenty to hand over for the game larder at Mansfield Park, and perhaps to give as gifts to local family, friends, and acquaintances.*

*Continued* ⇀

## SERVES 4

PREP + COOKING TIME: 25 MINUTES
+ 7–8 HOURS

2 hen pheasants or 1 hen and 1 small
   cock pheasant (ensure they will fit
   in the slow cooker pot)
2 tablespoons butter
1 tablespoon olive oil
2 onions, cut into wedges
4 oz. smoked bacon, diced
½ cup Madeira or extra chicken stock,
   if preferred
1 cup chicken stock
1 tablespoon red currant jelly
6 oz. mushrooms, sliced
3 thyme sprigs
salt and pepper

1. Preheat the slow cooker if necessary; see the
   manufacturer's instructions. Season inside the body
   cavity of each pheasant with salt and pepper.

2. Heat the butter and oil in a large skillet, add the
   pheasants, breast-side down, and fry over a medium
   heat until they are golden. Lift them out of the pan
   and put them on a plate.

3. Add the onion wedges and bacon to the pan and fry
   for 4–5 minutes, stirring, until golden. Pour in the
   Madeira, if using, stock, and red currant jelly, and
   bring to a boil, stirring, until the jelly has melted.
   Season with salt and pepper.

4. Add the pheasants to the slow cooker pot breast-side
   down. If they are very snug, you may need to put
   them into the pot sideways. Add the mushrooms and
   thyme sprigs, then pour in the hot onion mixture.

5. Cover with the lid and cook on low for 7–8 hours or
   until the meat is beginning to come away from the
   bones and the juices run clear when the pheasants
   are pierced through the thickest part with a skewer
   or small knife.

6. Lift the pheasants out of the slow cooker and place
   them on a large plate. Scoop out the onions, bacon,
   and mushrooms with a slotted spoon, place in a
   bowl, cover with foil, and keep hot. Strain the stock
   mixture into a large skillet and boil for 5–10 minutes
   until reduced and thickened.

7. Carve the breast meat and arrange it in shallow
   bowls. Spoon over the onion, bacon, and
   mushrooms, and serve with the sauce and mashed
   potatoes, and green cabbage, if desired.

# Chicken Curry

Ditch the takeout and try this fragrant chicken curry, full of aromatic spices, which is sure to become a family favorite. Serve it with steamed white or basmati rice with mango chutney on the side.

## SERVES 4

PREP + COOKING TIME: 45–50
    MINUTES

1 tablespoon olive oil

2 bay leaves

1 cinnamon stick

1 teaspoon ground cardamom

4 cloves

2 teaspoons cumin seeds

1 large onion, finely chopped

2 tablespoons finely grated garlic

2 tablespoons peeled and finely grated
    fresh ginger

1 tablespoon ground coriander

1 tablespoon ground cumin

14-oz. can chopped tomatoes

1¾ lb. skinless, boneless chicken
    thighs, cubed

1 teaspoon chili powder

1 cup water

½ cup plain yogurt, whisked

small handful chopped cilantro leaves

salt

1. Heat the oil in a large skillet over a high heat. When hot, add the bay leaves, cinnamon, cardamom, cloves, and cumin seeds. Stir-fry for 30 seconds until fragrant, then add the onion. Stir-fry for 4–5 minutes until the onion is soft.

2. Add the garlic, ginger, ground coriander, and cumin, and fry for 1 minute. Add the tomatoes and continue stir-frying for another minute.

3. Add the chicken, chili powder, and measured water. Season to taste and bring to a boil. Cover the pan, reduce the heat to medium-low, and simmer gently for 25 minutes, turning the chicken pieces now and then. Remove the pan from the heat and stir in the yogurt and cilantro.

*In a letter to her friend in Lesley Castle—one of Austen's juvenile skits—Charlotte Lutterell writes: "We spent a very pleasant Day, and had a very good Dinner, tho' to be sure the Veal was terribly underdone, and the Curry had no seasoning. I could not help wishing all dinner-time that I had been at the dressing of it."*

From the mid-eighteenth century on, the British East India Company controlled vast swathes of the Indian subcontinent, and its agents and employees gained a taste for the local cuisine, or at least a heavily Europeanized version of it. Back at home, "curries"—made with a curry powder blend rather than individual spices— became fashionable, along with Indian-inspired goods such as calico prints and fanciful Mughal-inspired buildings such as the Royal Pavilion (completed in 1823). The country's first Indian restaurant opened (briefly) in 1810, and there were even luxurious "Indian" baths, also in Brighton.

Miss Lutterell's curry sadly lacked seasoning—as a result it was as unlike a curry as a dish could be—so here we have gone for something more authentic, using a range of fresh, fragrant spices.

# Mrs. Bennet's Venison Pot

Richly savory and hearty, this great winter warmer is topped with crispy potato slices. You can use beef brisket or chuck roast here, in which case you may want to omit the bacon, as beef is not as lean as venison.

———————————

*T*oward the end of Pride and Prejudice, *Mrs. Bennet achieves a social coup: she manages to have the "two Netherfield gentlemen"—Mr. Bingley and Mr. Darcy—to dinner. The meal seems to set the seal on Mr. Bingley's proposing to her eldest daughter, Jane, and her feelings of triumph are compounded by her sense that she has also given her guests a very good meal: "The dinner was as well dressed as any I ever saw. The venison was roasted to a turn—and everybody said they never saw so fat a haunch."*

*Deer, like other game, were an important source of meat on a country estate, and a roast haunch was especially prized. Despite Mrs. Bennet's large family, we may imagine there was some meat left over from the dinner, and that, on the following day, she asked her cook to serve it in a rich, autumnal stew.*

## SERVES 6

PREP + COOKING TIME: 3 HOURS

2 tablespoons all-purpose flour

1¾ lb. lean stewing venison, cut into small pieces

10 juniper berries

3 tablespoons olive oil

1 cup diced bacon

1 large onion, chopped

3 carrots, sliced

½ teaspoon ground cloves

1¼ cups red wine

scant 1 cup chicken stock

1 tablespoon red wine vinegar

2 tablespoons red currant jelly

1½ cups vacuum-packed chestnuts

2 lb. large potatoes, thinly sliced

2 teaspoons chopped rosemary

3 tablespoons butter, softened

salt and black pepper

1. Season the flour with salt and pepper and use it to coat the venison. Crush the juniper berries using a mortar and pestle.

2. Heat the oil in a large, flameproof casserole dish and fry the meat in batches until browned, draining each batch to a plate. Add the bacon, onion, and carrots to the casserole dish and fry gently for 5 minutes or until browned.

3. Stir in the crushed juniper berries, cloves, wine, stock, vinegar, and red currant jelly and bring to a boil. Reduce the heat and stir in the chestnuts and venison.

4. Cover with a lid and cook in the oven at 325°F for 1 hour. Check the seasoning, then layer over the potato slices and return to the oven, covered, for an additional 30 minutes.

5. Blend the rosemary with the butter and a little seasoning and dot over the potatoes. Return to the oven, uncovered, for an additional 45 minutes or until the potatoes are lightly browned.

# Rabbit Stew

The secret to cooking rabbit is to do it slowly. Here it's cooked low and slow in a flavor-packed sauce to guarantee tender, juicy meat. If you can't get rabbit, use chicken thighs—but these won't have the same gamey flavor.

---

*E*ngland's game laws, instituted since Norman times, were extremely strict, forbidding the hunting of deer, rabbits, and other game to anyone who owned less than a certain amount of property, thereby depriving the vast majority of country dwellers of what might have been a cheap and plentiful source of meat. Harsh penalties were handed down on poachers who broke the laws, which only began to be relaxed from the 1830s.

*Only once in her novels does Jane Austen paint a brief portrait of the realities of life for many people in rural England, which were characterized by hard working conditions, poverty, illness, and want of education. Emma's "charitable visit" to a destitute family, the wretchedness of whose tumbledown cottage is matched by the wretchedness of their lives, is used to underline, despite her faults, the heroine's essential kindness and worth.*

*But set that aside, let Emma return to the luxuries of Hartfield, and imagine for a moment what the women of the cottage might have done with the brace of rabbit that Emma may well have left behind.*

*Continued* ⤙

## SERVES 4–6

PREP + COOKING TIME: 2 HOURS
  15 MINUTES

2 tablespoons butter

3 tablespoons olive oil

1 rabbit, cut into joints (ask your
    butcher to do this for you), or 3 lb.
    skinless chicken thighs

2 onions, thinly sliced

1 small celery stick, finely diced

pinch of crushed dried chilies

3 large rosemary sprigs

1 lemon, quartered

12 black olives

1½ cups dry white wine

1 cup chicken stock

salt

1. Melt the butter with the oil in a large, flameproof
   casserole dish with a tight-fitting lid large enough to
   hold the rabbit in a single layer. Lightly season the
   rabbit with salt and add to the pan with the onions,
   celery, crushed chilies, and rosemary. Cover and
   cook over a low heat for 1½ hours, turning the rabbit
   pieces every 30 minutes.

2. Uncover the pan, increase the heat to high, and boil
   until most of the juices released by the rabbit during
   cooking have evaporated. Add the lemon and olives,
   stir well, then pour in the wine. Bring to a boil and
   boil for 2 minutes, for the alcohol to evaporate.

3. Pour in the stock and simmer, turning and
   basting the rabbit occasionally, for an additional
   10–12 minutes until you have a rich, syrupy sauce.

# Mrs. Thorpe's Veal Pie

This is a delicious mix of curried meat, vegetables, and sweet golden raisins with a creamy golden topping. Hearty and comforting, it doesn't need any fancy sides—a crisp green salad is perfect.

---

## SERVES 4

PREP + COOKING TIME: 1 HOUR 15 MINUTES

2 tablespoons olive oil

1 lb. ground veal or pork

1 large onion, finely chopped

2 garlic cloves, crushed

2 tablespoons hot curry powder

3 tablespoons mango chutney

1⅓ cups fresh or frozen peas

1 large carrot, finely diced

½ cup golden raisins

1½ cups plain yogurt

4 large eggs

large handful of finely chopped cilantro leaves

salt and black pepper

1. Add the oil to a large nonstick skillet and place over a medium heat. Add the veal or pork and stir-fry for 2–3 minutes, stirring constantly, until the meat changes color. Add the onion and cook for an additional 4–5 minutes, stirring occasionally, until the onion starts to soften and the veal is lightly browned.

2. Add the garlic and curry powder, and fry for 1–2 minutes to allow the spices to cook. Remove the pan from the heat and stir in the mango chutney, peas, carrot, and golden raisins.

3. Spoon the mixture into a shallow ovenproof dish and press down well with the back of a spoon. Whisk the yogurt with the eggs, stir in the chopped cilantro, and season to taste. Pour over the meat to cover evenly. Cook in the oven at 350°F for 45–50 minutes until the mixture is piping hot and the top is set and golden.

*J*ane Austen is good at chatter—the seemingly inconsequential to-ings and fro-ings and en passants of everyday conversation. Here, in Northanger Abbey, we are eavesdropping on Mrs. Allen talking to Catherine Morland about her acquaintance in Bath and former schoolfellow, the widowed Mrs. Thorpe:

> *"Yes, I went to the pump-room as soon as you were gone, and there I met her, and we had a great deal of talk together. She says there was hardly any veal to be got at market this morning, it is so uncommonly scarce."*

This snippet may seem inconsequential, but in fact reveals something important about Mrs. Thorpe—that she lives in straitened enough circumstances that she herself has to go to the market to buy food for her large family. No wonder, then, that her eldest offspring, Isabella and John, are such inveterate fortune hunters. All the same, let's hope that Mrs. Thorpe eventually found her veal and was able to serve up this satisfying curried pie at the dinner table.

# Hunsford Parsonage Ginger Pork Chops

A brief stint marinating in the refrigerator gives these Asian-style pork chops a boost of flavor and tenderizes the meat. All this dish needs alongside it is a bowl of steamed white or brown rice.

---

## SERVES 4

PREP + COOKING TIME: 45 MINUTES

4 lean pork chops, about 5 oz. each

1½-inch piece of fresh ginger, peeled and grated

1 teaspoon sesame oil

1 tablespoon dark soy sauce

2 teaspoons preserved ginger syrup or honey

*For the dressing*

1½ tablespoons light soy sauce

juice of 1 blood orange

2 pieces of preserved ginger, finely chopped

*For the salad*

2 large carrots, peeled and coarsely grated

1 cup shredded snow peas

2 cups bean sprouts

2 scallions, thinly sliced

2 tablespoons unsalted peanuts, roughly chopped (optional)

1. Place the pork in a shallow, ovenproof dish and rub with the ginger, sesame oil, soy sauce, and preserved ginger syrup or honey until well covered. Leave to marinate for 10 minutes in the refrigerator.

2. Make the dressing. Mix together all the ingredients in a bowl and set aside for the flavors to develop. Cook the pork in the oven at 350°F for 18–20 minutes or until cooked through but still juicy.

3. Meanwhile, mix the carrots, snow peas, bean sprouts, and scallions in a large bowl. Just before serving, toss with the dressing and pile onto serving dishes. Sprinkle with the peanuts, if using, and top with the pork chops, drizzled with cooking juices. Serve immediately.

*I*n Pride and Prejudice, *on the day following Elizabeth Bennet and Maria Lucas's arrival at Hunsford Parsonage—the home of Mr. and Mrs. Collins—there is a sudden commotion in the household. Maria rushes up the stairs to Elizabeth's bedroom, breathless with excitement:*

*"Oh, my dear Eliza! pray make haste and come into the dining-room, for there is such a sight to be seen! I will not tell you what it is. Make haste, and come down this moment."*

*Elizabeth asked questions in vain; Maria would tell her nothing more, and down they ran into the dining-room, which fronted the lane, in quest of this wonder; it was two ladies stopping in a low phaeton at the garden gate.*

*"And is this all?" cried Elizabeth. "I expected at least that the pigs were got into the garden, and here is nothing but Lady Catherine and her daughter."*

Elizabeth is not just being facetious. In the countryside, it was commonplace for people of all classes to keep pigs. Fed on scraps from the kitchen, they, like poultry, were an important part of the household economy, and pork for the table was much prized. Here, too, is the kindly Mr. Woodhouse in Emma deliberating on what cut of pork should be sent to the impoverished Bates:

*"Hartfield pork is not like any other pork—but still it is pork—and, my dear Emma, unless one could be sure of their making it into steaks, nicely fried, as ours are fried, without the smallest grease, and not roast it, for no stomach can bear roast pork—I think we had better send the leg—do not you think so, my dear?"*

Back at Hunsford Parsonage, Mr. Collins—with a stronger stomach, it seems—likes his pork in the form of chops, marinated in ginger, then roasted in the oven.

# Chawton Cottage Garden Risotto

With deliciously sweet peas and delicate asparagus, this is a dish that sings of spring. Creamy without being too rich, it's sure to become a firm favorite. For a special treat, you could try serving it with juicy seared scallops.

*A*lthough rice continued to be a relatively expensive import in the Georgian era, *it featured widely in its cooking, used for both savory dishes and desserts like the perennially popular rice pudding. The latter, for example, makes a charming appearance in* Emma, *where the heroine, out and about in Highbury, comes across her two oldest nephews "whose healthy, glowing faces shewed all the benefit of a country run, and seemed to ensure a quick despatch of the roast mutton and rice pudding they were hastening home for."*

*Here we have come up with a savory rice dish inspired by Jane Austen's beautiful garden at Chawton. Imagine Jane and Cassandra wandering around the vegetable beds, picking the best asparagus spears and fattest pea pods for this fresh-tasting and summery risotto.*

## SERVES 4

PREP + COOKING TIME: **35** MINUTES

1 tablespoon olive oil

1 onion, finely chopped

1 garlic clove, crushed

1½ cups arborio rice

½ cup dry white wine

4¼ cups hot vegetable stock

1 cup roughly chopped fine asparagus
    spears

¾ cup frozen peas

2 tablespoons butter

salt and black pepper

*To serve*

1 cup arugula leaves

Parmesan or pecorino cheese shavings

1. Heat the oil in a large, heavy-based saucepan. Add the onion and cook for 5 minutes until softened. Add the garlic and rice and cook for 30 seconds until coated in the oil. Pour in the wine and bubble until boiled away.

2. Gradually add the stock, a ladleful at a time, stirring continuously and allowing each ladleful to be absorbed before adding the next. After 10 minutes, add the asparagus, then cook for an additional 5 minutes until the rice is tender.

3. Stir in the peas and butter, cover, and leave to stand for 1–2 minutes. Season the risotto to taste, then spoon into bowls and top each portion with some arugula and the Parmesan or pecorino shavings.

# A Potato and Cauliflower Curry

Add some spice to a midweek meal. Served spooned over bowls of steamed rice or with warmed naan and topped with vibrant green cilantro and thick yogurt, this healthy and easy curry is a great one-pan vegetarian main dish.

———————————————

*T*here was a gathering, if minor, movement of vegetarianism in Britain during Jane Austen's lifetime. In 1802 Joseph Ritson published An Essay on Abstinence from Animal Food, as a Moral Duty, and in 1812 Martha Brotherton produced the country's first vegetarian cookbook, Vegetable Cookery. These early vegetarian activists often supported animal rights as part of their wider radical, humanitarian ideals and tended to supplement their diets with a lot of dairy and eggs.

*We would look long and hard in Jane Austen's novels for any character remotely vegetarian—or indeed radical, but perhaps some of the more health-conscious inhabitants of the seaside resort in Sanditon, such as the Parker sisters, might have been persuaded to try this simple curry.*

## SERVES 4

PREP + COOKING TIME: **45** MINUTES

3 tablespoons vegetable oil

1 lb. potatoes, peeled and cut into bite-size chunks

1 large onion, roughly chopped

¼ cup medium curry paste

½ small cauliflower, cut into chunky florets

2 generous cups hot vegetable stock

1 cup frozen leaf spinach

*To serve*

chopped cilantro

thick plain yogurt

1. Heat the oil in a large deep-sided skillet or saucepan and cook the potato and onion over a medium heat for 5–6 minutes, stirring occasionally, until the vegetables are tinged with brown and begin to soften. Stir in the curry paste and cook for 1 minute to cook the spices.

2. Tip the cauliflower into the pan and stir to coat before adding the hot stock. Bring to a boil, then reduce the heat, cover, and simmer gently for about 15 minutes, stirring occasionally, until the potatoes and cauliflower are tender and the sauce has thickened.

3. Stir in the frozen spinach and cook for an additional 2–3 minutes until the spinach has wilted and the curry is hot. Sprinkle with the chopped cilantro and spoon over some yogurt to serve.

# Henry Tilney's Nice Mushroom Patties with the Nicest Onion Jelly

These juicy mushroom burgers are also ideal as a vegetarian barbecue option. If there's any of the sticky onion jelly left over, it's excellent with cheese and crackers or in a sandwich.

***

*Henry Tilney, in* Northanger Abbey, *is one of the most attractive of Austen's heroes—good-but-not-too-good-looking, witty, and considerate. And, unlike many of the novelist's young men, he turns out exactly as he first appears to be—the perfect marriage partner. He is, however, a bit of a know-it-all—see, for example, his only half-humorous lecture to Catherine Morland about the proper use of the word "nice" on their walk on the cliffs above Bath. The heroine has just described Ann Radcliffe's* The Mysteries of Udolpho *(1794) as "the nicest book in the world":*

> *"Very true . . . and this is a very nice day, and we are taking a very nice walk, and you are two very nice young ladies. Oh! It is a very nice word indeed! It does for everything. Originally perhaps it was applied only to express neatness, propriety, delicacy, or refinement—people were nice in their dress, in their sentiments, or their choice. But now every commendation on every subject is comprised in that one word."*

*At the risk of provoking Henry Tilney's satire, these mushroom patties, too, are nice, very nice, especially when served with the nicest onion jelly.*

## SERVES 4

PREP + COOKING TIME: **30–40** MINUTES, PLUS COOLING

8 large flat mushrooms, trimmed
1 tablespoon extra-virgin olive oil
4 ciabatta rolls
2 cups baby spinach leaves
salt and black pepper

*For the onion jelly*

¼ cup extra-virgin olive oil
4 onions, thinly sliced
4 thyme sprigs, lightly bruised
½ cup light brown sugar
scant ½ cup red wine vinegar
¼ cup red currant jelly

1. Make the onion jelly. Heat the oil in a saucepan and gently fry the onions, thyme sprigs, and some salt and pepper for 20–25 minutes until really soft and golden. Discard the thyme sprigs and stir in the sugar, vinegar, and red currant jelly. Simmer for 6–8 minutes until the sauce is thick and jellylike, then leave to cool completely.

2. Brush the mushrooms with the oil and season with salt and pepper. Cook under a preheated hot broiler for 2–3 minutes on each side. Meanwhile, toast the ciabatta rolls for about 1 minute on each side until lightly browned.

3. Fill each roll with two mushrooms and some spinach leaves and spoon in some onion jelly. Serve at once.

# Frank's Roast Vegetables

This is the easiest of accompaniments to a host of dishes, from roast chicken and sausages to broiled fish. Or, to make it a vegetarian main course, serve alongside some quinoa, perhaps with a little salty feta crumbled over it.

*T*hroughout *her letters Jane Austen shows her preoccupation with the family garden, especially the kitchen garden—with making sure that any prospective home had a good one, that the present one was well maintained and productive, and that there was a good (but not too expensive) gardener to run it. Here she is writing from Southampton, where from 1806 to 1809 she and her mother shared a house with her newly married brother Francis: "Our garden is putting in order by a man who bears a remarkably good character, has a very fine complexion, and asks something less than the first."*

*As a naval officer only too accustomed to the monotony of salted meat and ship's biscuits while out at sea, Francis Austen would surely have looked forward to fresh vegetables when home on leave (pages 108–109). After a long voyage, this simple tray of roasted vegetables, harvested by the ruddy-faced gardener just that morning, would have tasted like heaven.*

## SERVES 4

PREP + COOKING TIME: 1 HOUR 15 MINUTES

4 small potatoes, scrubbed

1 red onion

2 carrots

2 parsnips

8 garlic cloves, unpeeled

4 thyme sprigs

2 tablespoons extra-virgin olive oil

1. Cut the potatoes and onion into wedges and the carrots and parsnips into quarters. Put in a large roasting pan to fit in a single layer. Add the garlic cloves, thyme sprigs, oil, and salt and pepper, and stir well until evenly coated.

2. Roast in an oven at 425°F for 50–60 minutes until browned and tender, stirring halfway through.

# Mrs. Austen's Spinach and Potato Gratin

This simple dish is perfect for chilly days. It works well as a meat-free main dish, along with a green salad and perhaps some crusty bread, and would be delicious served alongside the Rabbit Stew (page 91).

*I*n the late eighteenth century, potatoes had yet to become the widespread crop and mainstay of the poor they were to become in the nineteenth. The novelist's mother, Mrs. Austen, was in this respect a pioneer in that she planted and dug up potatoes in her kitchen gardens at both Steventon and Chawton, and encouraged local people to follow her example, even if they proved hard to persuade. In this, she was following the recommendations of the Board of Agriculture, which recommended that farmers and cottagers plant potatoes to offset national wheat shortages.

## SERVES 4

PREP + COOKING TIME: 45 MINUTES

1¼ lb. potatoes, peeled and thinly sliced
10 cups spinach leaves
1¾ cups shredded mozzarella cheese
4 tomatoes, sliced
3 eggs, beaten
1¼ cups light cream
salt and black pepper

1. Cook the potatoes in a large saucepan of salted boiling water for 5 minutes, then drain well.

2. Meanwhile, in a separate saucepan of boiling water, cook the spinach for 1–2 minutes until just wilted. Drain and squeeze out the excess water.

3. Grease a large, ovenproof dish and line the base with half the potato slices. Cover with the spinach and half the mozzarella, seasoning each layer well with salt and pepper. Cover with the remaining potato slices and arrange the tomato slices on top. Sprinkle with the remaining mozzarella.

4. Whisk together the eggs and cream in a bowl and season with salt and pepper. Pour over the ingredients in the dish.

5. Bake at 350°F for about 30 minutes until bubbling and golden. Serve immediately.

# Food at Sea

Two of Jane Austen's brothers served in the Royal Navy. Francis William Austen (1774–1865) served as an officer and later captain during the Napoleonic Wars (1803–15) and eventually rose to become Admiral of the Fleet. His younger brother, Charles John Austen (1779–1852), also served as a Royal Naval officer, and, like his brother, was involved in the capture of many French ships. Charles, too, had a distinguished career, rising to become a rear admiral. Beyond childhood, the novelist knew her brothers only during their days as officers and captains (she did not live long enough to witness their ultimate promotions). For several years before the move to Chawton in 1809, she lived with her brother "Frank" and his family in the important naval port of Southampton, so she must have been used to thrilling tales of engagements at sea as well as with more mundane accounts of everyday maritime life, including the monotony of the food.

Austen gives a sympathetic portrayal of the navy officers in her last completed novel, Persuasion (1817), set just after the end of the wars. Admiral and Mrs. Croft, Captain Harville and his wife, and, of course, the novel's hero, Captain Wentworth, are all shown as practical, honest, warm, and energetic—self-made people who have served their country loyally and made their fortunes to boot, offering an unflattering contrast with the self-entitled, self-serving gentry, as represented by Sir Walter Elliot and his ilk. Captain Wentworth provides brief snippets of his life at sea to the Musgrove family, sailing to the West Indies and back on board the Asp, his first command. The captain even permits himself to criticize the state of his ship—described as "quite worn out and broken up"—and, by extension, the Admiralty which sent it out on service:

> "The Admiralty," [Wentworth] continued, "entertain themselves now and then, with sending a few hundred men to sea, in a ship not fit to be employed. But they have a great many to provide for; and among the thousands that may just as well go to the bottom as not, it is impossible for them to distinguish the very set who may be least missed."

Wentworth's (and Austen's) sympathy for the conditions faced by ordinary sailors is tantalizingly hinted at here. How were, we may wonder, the thousands "provided for," in terms of the food that kept them, hopefully, fit and healthy during their many weeks at sea? Let's join Captain Wentworth on board the Asp for a while, as he sets sail from—let's presume—Southampton, on his way to the West Indies—a passage of about a month or so, in more or less good conditions.

Initially, there may well have been some fresh provisions on board—fresh meat and vegetables—but these would very quickly have been replaced with the standard rations. The Royal Navy was in fact rather strict about these—a well-nourished crew, after all, meant an efficient and non-mutinous one—but the kind and quality of the food was dictated by the conditions on board and the length of time at sea, at a time when there was no widespread method of food preservation other than brining (canning was in its earliest infancy). The bulk of the sailor's rations was provided by the infamous ship's biscuit—later known as hardtack—of which a mighty pound (0.45 kg) was (theoretically) issued to every sailor every day. Unappetizing and tooth-breakingly hard at the beginning of the voyage, the biscuits soon came under attack from weevils, so that it was customary to give them a sharp tap before dipping them into drink to soften them a little. To this was added a ration of salt pork (Sunday and Thursday) or salt beef (Tuesday and Saturday), both served up with a slop of grayish cooked dried peas. On the other days of the week there was a pint of oatmeal, plus a bit of butter and cheese. Alcohol—in the form of beer, wine, and rum—featured heavily.

Captain Wentworth and his officers would have fared somewhat better, supplementing their rations (or even replacing them) with personal provisions, though with the same limitations on storage and preservation. As the port of St. John's, on Antigua, at last came into sight, the good captain would surely have felt the same elation as the rest of his men as they looked forward to a safe harbor, dry land, and meals of fresh meat, bread, eggs, and vegetables.

# Trash & Sweet Things:

## Ices,
## Cakes &
## Puddings

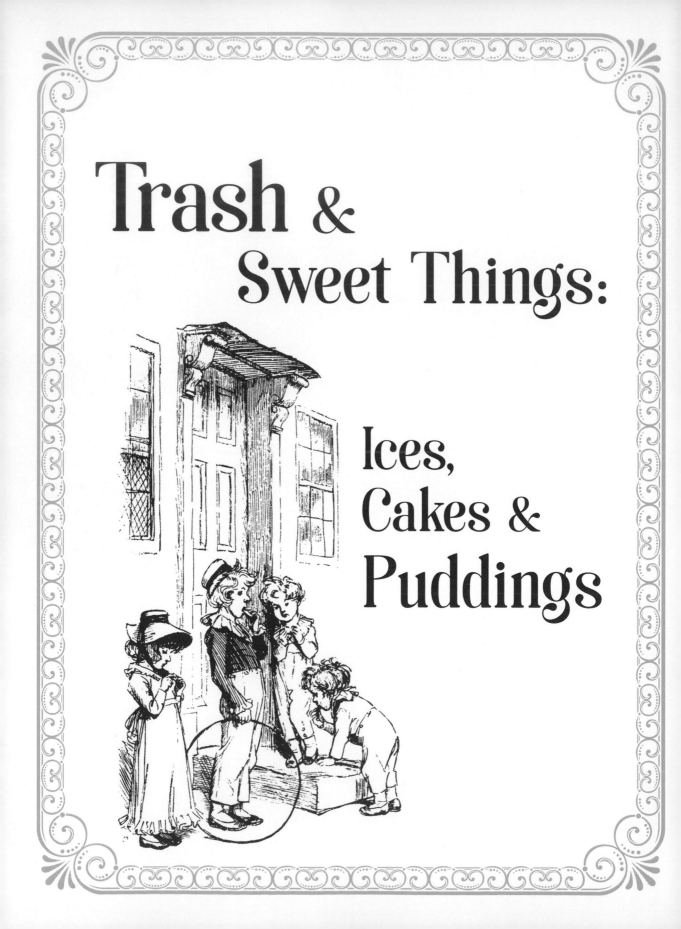

*I*n Persuasion, *one of the many bones of contention between querulous young mother Mary Musgrove—the sister of the book's heroine, Anne Elliot—and her mother-in-law who lives up at the Great House is that every time her children go up to see their grandmother, she spoils them rotten by giving them too much "trash and sweet things." Mary complains to Anne that "she humours and indulges them to such a degree . . . that they are sure to come back sick and cross for the rest of the day."*

*Mary Musgrove is being mocked here, but Jane Austen no doubt shared Mary's worries about overindulging children—our sensible writer is always in favor of moderation in all things. On the other hand, she certainly did not disapprove of cakes and "sweet things." By her own admission, she had an eye for a good cake, though as ever it is always hard to know whether she has her tongue firmly in her cheek: in a letter to her sister Cassandra written July 15, 1808, she describes a visit to a bakery and adds, "You know how interesting the purchase of a sponge-cake is to me."*

*In the homes of the very wealthy, all moderation went out of the window when it came to the dessert course of a formal dinner—on the freshly laid table might be exotic, hothouse-raised fruits, arranged in pyramids—as Elizabeth Bennet witnesses at Mr. Darcy's stately home in Derbyshire; sugar-paste sculptures of flowers and cherubs; ices served in fantastic architectural shapes; and a profusion of cookies, macaroons, and other delicacies—all served with sweet dessert wines.*

*In the twenty-first century we might be happier with the more impoverished Dashwoods' take on the final course (still laid out by a servant, we note): "When the dessert and the wine were arranged, and Mrs. Dashwood and Elinor were left by themselves, they remained long together in a similarity of thoughtfulness and silence."*

# Whipt Syllabub

Cream and wine combine beautifully in this quintessentially English dessert. It's a delicate, creamy, and indulgent way to end a meal. You can serve it with shortcake or lemon cookies for contrasting crunch if you like.

---

*Syllabub—a glorious concoction of cream, wine, sugar, and lemon—was clearly a great treat in the young Jane Austen's life, as it turns up twice in letters in her unfinished novel Lesley Castle, written perhaps in 1792 when she was just sixteen. In one of the letters, Miss Charlotte Lutterell writes of how her sister has run up to her to impart some bad news, "her face as White as a Whipt syllabub," and, in another, her friend Miss Margaret Lesley writes of her brother that he has a heart "as delicate as sweet and as tender as a Whipt-Syllabub." Both instances perfectly sum up the attraction of a well-made syllabub—a glass of pale, sugary, frothy scrumptiousness, with an alcoholic kick to boot—childish and adult all at the same time.*

## SERVES 4

PREP TIME: **10** MINUTES

1¼ cups heavy cream
⅓ cup sweet white wine
¼ cup superfine sugar
finely grated zest and juice of ½ lemon

1. Whisk the cream in a clean bowl with a handheld electric whisk until it just starts to hold its shape.

2. Add the wine, a third at a time, whisking well between each addition to ensure the mixture is well combined.

3. Stir in the sugar and lemon juice and continue whisking until fluffy and thick. Spoon into glasses, sprinkle with lemon zest, and serve.

# Summer Berry Delice

This one does take a little time, but the results are worth it. And it's perfect for when you are entertaining as it can be prepared well in advance, leaving you free to get on with other things in the kitchen. You will need six 3-inch round molds that you can use to layer the cake and the mousse, or you can cut strips of baking acetate plastic to create your own molds.

*T*he strawberry-gathering party at Donwell Abbey is one of the most memorable scenes in Emma. As Mr. Knightley's guests busy themselves about the strawberry beds, Austen gives us a smattering of the conversation that passes among them—a conversation led, it seems, by the self-important vicar's wife, Mrs. Elton, the self-appointed hostess of the party. In it we find a kind of summary of the idées reçues, "received ideas," about strawberries in Regency England:

> The best fruit in England—every body's favorite—always wholesome.—These the finest beds and finest sorts.—Delightful to gather for one's self—the only way of really enjoying them.—Morning decidedly the best time—never tired—every sort good—hautboy infinitely superior—no comparison—the others hardly eatable—hautboys very scarce—Chili preferred—white wood finest flavor of all . . .

The white wood and hautboy were two native species (the Alpine and musk strawberry, respectively), while the Chili was a new strawberry from South America, as the name implies.

Mrs. Elton, despite being "never tired" of strawberry picking, very quickly flags in the heat and goes to sit in the shade. Perhaps one of these light-as-a-feather delices would have offered her some refreshment and comfort.

*Continued* ↪

## SERVES 6

PREP + COOKING TIME: 1 HOUR,
PLUS COOLING AND CHILLING

3 eggs
⅓ cup superfine sugar
generous ½ cup all-purpose flour,
    sifted

*For the mousse*

2 teaspoons powdered gelatin
2 tablespoons cold water
2 egg whites
⅓ cup superfine sugar
⅔ cup heavy cream
generous 1 cup frozen summer fruits,
    just thawed, pureed

*To decorate*

a few whole red currants and
    raspberries and some strawberries,
    halved
a few small mint leaves
confectioners' sugar, for dusting

1. Whisk the eggs and sugar until they are very thick and the whisk leaves a trail when lifted. Gently fold in the flour. Line the base and sides of a cake pan with a base of 14 x 10 inches. Pour in the mixture.

2. Bake at 350°F for 12–15 minutes until the cake is golden and springs back when pressed. Leave to cool in the pan.

3. If you are using round molds to layer the delices, cut twelve circles from the cake and remove the excess. Place the molds back over six of the cake circles and set aside.

4. If you are using baking acetate plastic to create the molds, cut twelve 3-inch circles of cake using a cookie cutter. Cut strips of the acetate measuring 11 x 3 inches. Wrap a strip tightly around six of the cake circles and secure with tape. Put on a cookie sheet.

5. Sprinkle gelatin over the measured water in a bowl and leave to soak for 5 minutes. Stand the bowl in a pan of simmering water and leave until the gelatin has dissolved to a clear liquid. Whisk the egg whites until stiff peaks form, then gradually whisk in the sugar until thick and glossy. Whip the cream in a second bowl. Trickle the gelatin into the cream and mix together, then fold in the fruit puree and egg mixture.

6. Divide the mixture between the molds, then top with the remaining cake circles. Chill the mousses for 4–5 hours until set. Remove the delices from the molds, sprinkle each one with a few whole or halved berries, a couple of small mint leaves, dust with sifted confectioners' sugar, and serve.

# Mr. Woodhouse's "All-Apple" Tarts

Using store-bought puff pastry, these look super impressive but are a breeze to make. You can use any other fruit instead of apples—plums, apricots, and cherries would all work well. If you're in a hurry, skip the apricot glaze and dust them with confectioners' sugar instead.

---

*In the village of Highbury, Emma's Mr. Woodhouse always has the last word on what is healthy and unhealthy when it comes to food, and, perhaps surprisingly, apple tart is one of the dishes that passes muster, if eaten in moderation. "Let Emma help you," he tells his guest Miss Bates, "to a little bit of tart—a very little bit. Ours are all apple-tarts. You need not be afraid of unwholesome preserves here. I do not advise the custard."*

*In the following recipe, we have followed Mr. Woodhouse's strictures to a T, excepting a little apricot glaze to add a tempting sheen to the sliced apples. We agree about the custard, too, though a scoop of vanilla ice cream never did anyone much harm.*

## MAKES 4

PREP + COOKING TIME: 55 MINUTES,
PLUS CHILLING

12 oz. ready-made puff pastry

2 crisp green dessert apples (such as Granny Smith), peeled, cored, and sliced

1 tablespoon superfine sugar

2 tablespoons unsalted butter, chilled

sour cream, to serve

*For the apricot glaze*

¾ cup apricot jelly

2 teaspoons lemon juice

2 teaspoons water

1. Cut the pastry into four, then roll out each piece on a lightly floured surface to ⅛ inch thick. Cut out four circles using a 5-inch plate as a guide—make a number of short cuts around the plate rather than drawing the knife around, which can stretch the pastry. Place on a cookie sheet.

2. Place a slightly smaller plate on each pastry circle and score around the edge to form a ¾-inch border. Prick the centers with a fork and chill for 30 minutes.

3. Arrange the apple slices in a circle over the pastry rounds and sprinkle with the sugar. Grate the butter over the top and bake at 425°F for 25–30 minutes until the pastry and apples are golden.

4. Put the jelly in a small saucepan with the lemon juice and the measured water and heat gently until the jelly melts. Increase the heat and boil for 1 minute, remove from the heat, and press through a fine sieve. Keep warm, then brush over each apple tart while they are still warm.

# Mrs. Elton's Ice

Take a break from the heat with this tangy, icy, and refreshing recipe, with its light texture and vibrant flavor. The bay leaf may seem an odd addition, but it complements the lemon really well and makes such a difference to the taste.

*I*n Emma *Mrs. Elton, the vicar's snobbish new wife, declares herself a "little shocked" when she first arrives in the provincial village of Highbury. Used to Bath and London ways, she is quick to pinpoint the ways in which village society falls short of fashionable urban norms, one of which is the astounding fact of "there being no [water] ice at Highbury card parties."*

*Ice cream and water ices, as we have seen, were indeed the height of fashion in Georgian society, but depended of course on the availability of large quantities of ice for churning—something available only to the very rich who might maintain an icehouse on their estate. This simple lemon-and-honey ice may well have satisfied Mrs. Elton's taste for the high life until her next visit to Bath.*

## SERVES 4–6

PREP + COOKING TIME: 25 MINUTES,
PLUS COOLING AND FREEZING

4 large or 6 medium lemons

¼ cup water

2 tablespoons honey

¼ cup superfine sugar

1 bay leaf or lemon balm sprig

2 cups plain yogurt

strips of lemon peel, to decorate

1. Slice off the top of each lemon. Carefully scoop out all the pulp and juice with a teaspoon. Discard any white pith, skin, and pits (take care to remove all the white pith, as it will leave the ice tasting bitter), then puree the pulp and juice in a food processor or blender. You will need ⅔ cup. If there is less than this, top it up with water.

2. Put the measured water, honey, sugar, and bay leaf into a saucepan. Stir over a low heat until the sugar has dissolved, then leave to cool. Blend the mixture with the lemon puree and the yogurt. Do not remove the herb at this stage.

3. Pour into a shallow dish and freeze until lightly frozen, then gently fork the mixture and remove the herb. Return the ice to the freezer.

4. Transfer the ice to the refrigerator about 20 minutes before serving. Serve in individual bowls, decorated with strips of lemon peel.

# Godmersham Melon Sorbet

This summery, palate-cleansing sorbet can also be made using honeydew melon or watermelon. For a pretty-as-a-picture bowl of icy treats, make three batches, each using a different melon, and serve a different-colored scoop of each.

*Water ice and ice creams were the height of fashion in the late eighteenth and early nineteenth century, and like almost all fashions they were expensive, the preserve of the elite. While staying with her wealthy brother, Edward Austen Knight (1767–1852), at Godmersham Park, Kent, in the summer of 1808, Jane Austen declared her intention of devoting herself to "Elegance & Ease & Luxury . . . I shall eat Ice & drink French wine, & be above Vulgar Economy." Ices (and a wine cellar) were well beyond Mrs. Austen and her daughters' means, but for their brother—who could afford to maintain an icehouse on his Kentish estate—they were an almost everyday luxury. Edward would also have had the space, the manpower, and the hothouses needed to raise fruit like melons through much of the year—so something akin to our refreshing sorbet may well have featured on the Godmersham menu.*

## SERVES 4–6

PREP TIME: 15 MINUTES, PLUS FREEZING

1 cantaloupe melon, weighing about
    2 lb., seeds discarded and flesh
    scooped out
⅓ cup confectioners' sugar
juice of 1 lime or small lemon
1 egg white

1. Place the melon flesh in a food processor or blender with the confectioners' sugar and lime or lemon juice, and process to a puree. (Alternatively, rub through a sieve.) Pour into a freezer container, cover, and freeze for 2–3 hours. If using an ice-cream maker, puree and then pour into the machine, churn, and freeze until half-frozen.

2. Whisk the melon mixture to break up the ice crystals, then whisk the egg white until stiff and whisk it into the half-frozen melon mixture. Return to the freezer until firm. Alternatively, add whisked egg white to the ice-cream machine and churn until very thick.

3. Transfer the sorbet to the refrigerator 20 minutes before serving to soften slightly or scoop straight from the ice-cream machine. Scoop the sorbet into glass dishes to serve.

# Cherry Almond Ice Cream

This is a lovely combination of sweet fresh cherries—choose the darkest, ripest ones you can find—cream, and crunchy almonds. For a boozy version, you could add a dash of Amaretto to the mixture. Serve with almond biscotti and perhaps with a few fresh, whole cherries to decorate.

## SERVES 6

PREP + COOKING TIME: 40 MINUTES, PLUS COOLING AND FREEZING

⅔ cup milk

⅔ cup almond flour

1 egg

1 egg yolk

⅓ cup superfine sugar

2–3 drops almond extract

1 lb. red cherries, pitted

¼ cup slivered almonds

⅔ cup heavy cream

1. Pour the milk into a small saucepan and stir in the almond flour. Bring to a boil, then set aside.

2. Put the egg and the yolk into a heatproof bowl with the sugar and beat until pale and thick. Add the milk and almond mixture. Place the bowl over a pan of gently simmering water and stir until thick. Stir in the almond extract and leave to cool.

3. Puree the cherries in a food processor or blender, then stir into the custard.

4. Toss the slivered almonds in a pan over a low heat to toast them. Leave to cool.

5. Whip the cream until it forms soft peaks. Fold the whipped cream into the cherry mixture.

6. Transfer the mixture to a freezer container, cover, and freeze until firm, beating twice at hourly intervals. Stir the slivered almonds into the mixture at the last beating. (If using an ice-cream machine, pour the cherry mixture into the machine, add the cream, churn, and freeze. Once frozen, fold in the slivered almonds.)

7. Serve two to three scoops of the ice cream in individual glasses.

*T*he ices and ice creams of the Georgian era came in a wide range of flavors, many of which we would recognize today, though one or two—such as Parmesan ice cream or burnt ice cream—might cause some of us to raise an eyebrow. Frederick Nutt's The Complete Confectioner (1789) gives recipes for no fewer than thirty-two ice creams and twenty-four ices, made with fresh fruit, jellies, or essences such as bergamot. Floral flavorings such as elderflower and rose were popular, as were ices fortified with alcohol such as rum.

At dinner, such ices might be served in a pretty porcelain seau à glace (ice cream pail) or, later in the period, in elaborate molded shapes such as fruits and vegetables and seashells. This ice cream is delicious enough, however, to need nothing more complicated than a sundae glass to sit in, perhaps with one or two Ratafias (page 126) on the side.

# Lydia's Whim-Wham

These super-speedy, super-easy trifles use store-bought cake and custard, but you could use the Pound Cake recipe (page 26) and make your own custard instead. If you are making these for children, replace the sherry with orange juice.

---

*T*he dramatic climax of Pride and Prejudice *occurs offstage, so to speak—Lydia Bennet and George Wickham's scandalous elopement to Gretna Green, across the Scottish border, is reported to her father in a letter written by Colonel Forster, with whom the youngest of the Bennet sisters has been staying in Brighton. Lydia is rather proud of her adventures than otherwise, and we can imagine her telling her sisters about her indelicate trip to Scotland with some glee.*

*And what might have the newlyweds have dined upon on their wedding night? Perhaps a dish of haggis and neeps and tatties and the whiskey-flavored trifle known as a whim-wham, a term applied in the eighteenth century to any fanciful thing. What more perfect concoction for the Lydia Bennets of this world?*

## SERVES 6

PREP + COOKING TIME: 20 MINUTES

3½ oz. white chocolate, broken into
    small pieces
⅓ cup whiskey
1 store-bought pound cake, about
    10 oz., cut into 6 slices
generous ¾ cup mascarpone cheese
½ cup heavy cream
1 tablespoon superfine sugar
¼ teaspoon vanilla extract
⅔ cup store-bought fresh thick custard
2½ cups raspberries
white chocolate curls or shavings, to
    decorate

1. Melt the chocolate in a heatproof bowl set over a saucepan of gently simmering water, ensuring the bowl does not touch the water, then leave to cool.

2. Meanwhile, pour the whiskey into a shallow bowl and dip in each of the cake slices to just dampen. Place in six serving dishes and set aside.

3. Place the mascarpone, cream, sugar, and vanilla extract in a large bowl and beat with a handheld electric whisk until thick. Fold in the cooled chocolate and custard.

4. Sprinkle half of the raspberries over the soaked cake slices, then spoon over the custard cream.

5. Sprinkle with the remaining raspberries and serve decorated with white chocolate curls or shavings.

# Devizes Cheesecakes

These individual cheesecakes are super easy to make but look impressive. Change things up by varying the base—try gingersnaps or shortbread cookies—and the accompaniments: strawberries, mango, and blueberries all work well.

---

*I*n May 1799, Austen wrote to her sister, Cassandra, "Our journey yesterday went off exceedingly well, nothing occurred to alarm or delay us . . . At Devizes we had comfortable rooms and a good dinner, to which we sat down about five; amongst other things we had asparagus and a lobster, which made me wish for you, and some cheesecakes, on which the children made so delightful a supper as to endear the town of Devizes to them for a long time."

*Austen is good at painting pictures of domestic contentment—she certainly knew that happiness lies in small things, and undoubtedly that one of those small things was cheesecake. The cheesecake of the period was somewhat akin to an almond-thickened custard baked in a pastry case, but we think this more modern take on the cheesecake would have pleased the Austen children just as well.*

## SERVES 6

PREP + COOKING TIME: **30** MINUTES

1 cup graham cracker crumbs
2 tablespoons unsalted butter, melted
generous ¾ cup cream cheese
¼ cup superfine sugar
¼ cup sour cream
finely grated zest of ½ lemon
1 teaspoon vanilla extract
1 tablespoon cornstarch
2 eggs
raspberries, to serve
confectioners' sugar, for dusting

1. Line a 6-hole muffin pan with paper cases. Stir the graham cracker crumbs into the melted butter and press into the bases of the cases. Chill while you make the filling.

2. Place the cream cheese, sugar, sour cream, lemon zest, vanilla extract, cornstarch, and eggs in a bowl and beat together.

3. Spoon the mixture over the graham cracker bases and bake at 325°F for 20 minutes. Leave to cool in the pan for 5 minutes.

4. Remove the cheesecakes from the cases and place on a serving plate. Serve warm, decorated with raspberries and a dusting of confectioners' sugar.

# Martha Lloyd's Ratafia Cakes

These easy-to-make macaroons are sure to become a go-to recipe. You can make a chocolate version by replacing ¼ cup of the almond flour with ¼ cup cocoa powder and decorating with zigzags of melted chocolate drizzled over with a teaspoon, rather than the blanched almonds.

———————————

*Ratafia cakes seem to have been a regular fixture in the Austen household at Chawton—at least, they make an appearance in the receipt book kept by Martha Lloyd (1765–1843), who lived with the Austens at Chawton and was Jane's closest friend after Cassandra—virtually a second sister. The cookies—which were very like modern macaroons—took their name from Ratafia, a bitter almond liqueur, alongside which they might be served as a light refreshment during the evening, perhaps during a game of Vingt-Un or Commerce.*

## MAKES ABOUT 15

PREP + COOKING TIME: 25 MINUTES

2 egg whites
½ cup superfine sugar
1 cup almond flour
½ teaspoon orange flower water
    (optional)
blanched almonds, to decorate

1. Whisk the egg whites in a clean bowl with a handheld electric whisk until soft peaks form. Gradually whisk in the sugar, a spoonful at a time, until thick and glossy. Add the almond flour and the orange flower water, if using, and stir until combined.

2. Drop rounded teaspoonfuls of the mixture, slightly apart, on a large cookie sheet lined with parchment paper. Press an almond on top of each.

3. Bake at 350°F for about 15 minutes until the macaroons are pale golden and just crisp. Leave on the paper for 5 minutes, then transfer to a wire rack to cool.

# Chawton Cottage Plum Pudding

As nights draw in, we yearn for warm, soothing desserts, and this slow cooker recipe, which showcases fall's bounty of blackberries and plums, is just the thing. Serve with steaming hot custard poured over, and dig in.

*J*ane Austen loved the garden at Chawton. She wrote passionately and knowledgeably about it in her letters to her sister, Cassandra, charting its abundance of trees, shrubs, and flowers as they passed through their seasonal changes. Summer was a time of particular delight for her. In one letter she writes:

> Our young Piony at the foot of the Fir tree has just blown & looks very handsome & the whole of the Shrubbery Border will soon be very gay with Pinks & Sweet Williams, in addition to the Columbines already in bloom. The Syringas too are coming out . . .

But Austen was well aware that a garden was about much more than sensual splendor; it also had to play its part in the household economy. Thus she continues:

> We are likely to have a great crop of Orleans plumbs–but not many greengages– on the standard scarcely any–three or four dozen perhaps against the wall.

In Chawton Cottage's thriving plum trees was the promise, she saw, of jellies and desserts in the coming months, and bottled fruits through the winter. Here is a recipe that will capture all the freshness of those "Orleans plumbs" but sturdy enough to keep away any fall chill.

Continued ⇝

## SERVES 6

PREP + COOKING TIME:
4½–5½ HOURS

7 tablespoons butter, at room
    temperature, plus extra for greasing

¾ cup blackberries

7 oz. ripe red plums, halved, pitted,
    and sliced

2 tablespoons raspberry jelly

½ cup superfine sugar

¾ cup self-rising flour

2 eggs, beaten

⅔ cup almond flour

few drops of almond extract

toasted slivered almonds, to decorate
    (optional)

1. Preheat the slow cooker if necessary; see the manufacturer's instructions. Lightly butter a 5-cup soufflé dish and line the base with a circle of nonstick parchment paper, checking first that the dish will fit in the slow cooker pot. Arrange the blackberries and plums in the base, then dot with the jelly.

2. Beat the butter and sugar in a bowl with a wooden spoon or handheld electric whisk until soft and creamy. Gradually mix in alternate spoonfuls of flour and beaten egg, and continue adding and beating until the mixture is smooth. Stir in the almond flour and almond extract. Spoon the mixture over the fruit, spread it level, and cover the top with foil.

3. Lower the dish into the slow cooker pot and pour boiling water into the pot to come halfway up the sides of the dish. Cover with the lid and cook on high for 4–5 hours or until the cake is well risen and springs back when pressed with a fingertip.

4. Lift the dish out of the slow cooker pot using a dish towel and remove the foil. Loosen the edges of the dessert with a knife and turn out onto a plate with a rim. Decorate with toasted slivered almonds, if desired.

# Mrs. Weston's Wedding Cake

For an extra-indulgent version of this rich, dense cake, top it with whipped cream and slices of banana, and drizzle caramel sauce over. If you want to make it ahead, it can be frozen for one month, well wrapped, at the end of step 2. Thaw and continue with steps 3 and 4.

## SERVES 8–10

PREP + COOKING TIME: **50** MINUTES, PLUS COOLING

5 eggs
generous ¾ cup superfine sugar
1 teaspoon vanilla extract
1¼ cups all-purpose flour
2 teaspoons baking powder
9 tablespoons butter, melted
scant 1 cup sweetened condensed milk
scant 1 cup evaporated milk
scant 1 cup milk

*To decorate*

1 cup heavy cream
1 tablespoon superfine sugar
selection of fruit, such as strawberries,
    blueberries, and oranges

1. Beat together the eggs and sugar in a bowl until pale and thickened. Add the vanilla extract, then gradually stir in the flour and baking powder. Carefully stir in the melted butter until well combined.

2. Pour the mixture into a lightly greased and lined 9-inch cake pan. Bake at 350°F for 30–35 minutes until golden and a skewer inserted into the center comes out clean.

3. Whisk together all three milks in a bowl. Prick all over the warm cake with a skewer, then spoon over the milk mixture, letting it sink in. Leave to cool.

4. When ready to serve, whisk together the cream and sugar in a bowl until soft peaks form. Spoon over the cake, then top with the fruit.

**E**mma *begins and ends with weddings. The first wedding, which takes place just before the narrative opens, is between Emma's former governess, Miss Taylor, and Mr. Weston, an ex-military man who has a small estate close to Highbury. Georgian marriages were held relatively early in the day, after which the couple and the guests would share a relatively simple wedding meal that was quite literally a breakfast—featuring hot rolls, eggs, ham, coffee, and chocolate. The wedding cake was a relative latecomer to this small-scale feast, and was intended as much for friends and relatives who had been unable to come as for those who had, sent around in paper packages.*

*In Chapter 2 of* Emma, *Mr. Woodhouse is much preoccupied with Mrs. Weston's wedding cake—in part because he worries that its richness will "disagree with many" and in part, we surmise, because it is a symbol of a change in his home circumstances that he would prefer not to have happened. Mr. Woodhouse might have made an exception for the following very simple celebration cake—though no doubt his own daughter's wedding cake would have been a much grander affair, looking toward the towering confections of the Victorian era.*

# Gingerbread Loaf

This old-fashioned favorite is a cake loved by kids and adults alike. Dark, soft, and squidgy, the addition of molasses gives real depth of flavor while the modern twist of pomegranate seeds adorn the top like pretty jewels.

*Ginger has had an important place in European cooking since at least medieval times and, along with pepper and cinnamon, was considered one of the "major" spices. Candied or preserved ginger was an especial treat and was often given as a present. The taste for ginger was still very much alive in Georgian times when jars of homemade preserved ginger would have been a staple of any respectable larder. In an 1808 letter to her sister, Jane Austen describes how a very dull evening entertaining guests in their Southampton home, just before Christmas, was relieved by the late appearance of a tray of widgeon (a kind of duck) and preserved ginger (which were both, she confides, "as delicious as one could wish")—a common Regency yuletide treat.*

*Preserved ginger would have turned up in sweet as well as savory dishes. Here, accordingly, is a rich, dark gingerbread that Jane Austen would have enjoyed. You needn't feel ashamed of using store-bought preserved ginger here.*

## SERVES 10

PREP + COOKING TIME: 1 HOUR 20 MINUTES

⅓ cup unsalted butter, plus extra for greasing

1¾ cups all-purpose flour

1 teaspoon baking soda

6 tablespoons milk

1 egg

½ cup dark brown sugar

⅓ cup molasses

3 pieces of preserved stem ginger in syrup, chopped

1¼ cups pomegranate juice

2 tablespoons honey

1 pomegranate

1. Grease and line 2 loaf pans, each approximately 8 x 3¼ inches, with nonstick parchment paper.

2. Sift the flour and baking soda into a bowl. Beat together the milk and egg. Put the sugar, molasses, and butter in a saucepan and heat gently until the butter melts and the sugar dissolves. Remove from the heat and add to the milk mixture along with the chopped ginger. Add to the dry ingredients and stir well until combined using a large metal spoon. Turn into the pans and level the surface.

3. Bake at 325°F for 30 minutes, or until just firm to the touch and a skewer inserted in the center comes out clean. Once cool, turn out onto a wire rack.

4. In a saucepan, boil the pomegranate juice for about 15 minutes until thick and syrupy and reduced to about 3 tablespoons. Stir in the honey. Halve the pomegranate and push the halves inside out to release the fleshy seeds, discarding any white membrane, and sprinkle over the cakes. Drizzle with the syrup and cut into small squares to serve.

# Seashell Valentines

These delicate little treats with their distinctive scalloped shell shape have been given a twist by adding macadamia nuts and maple syrup. You can serve them with maple syrup, as suggested, or simply dust with confectioners' sugar. Either way, they're best eaten the day they are made, preferably still warm.

———————————————

**P**ersuasion *(1817) is many readers' favorite among Jane Austen's novels: its tender fall tone, the technical virtuosity of the writing, and its sympathetic portrayal of a social class—the naval heroes of the Napoleonic Wars and their families—beyond the country gentry that provided the usual milieu of Jane Austen's fiction seem to herald a fresh, more outward-looking direction in her work. Above all, however, it is the sheer likability of the two central characters, Anne Elliot and Captain Frederick Wentworth, and the fact that Austen gives them a second chance in life, despite their "advanced" years (Anne is twenty-seven and Frederick in his early thirties), that makes the novel so deeply moving.*

*Here are some lovely little cakes that celebrate the belated marriage and rediscovered love of Anne and Frederick—God bless the bride and groom!*

## MAKES 18

PREP + COOKING TIME: 25 MINUTES,
  PLUS STANDING

2 large eggs

½ cup superfine sugar

2 tablespoons maple syrup, plus extra to serve (optional)

pinch of salt

1 cup all-purpose flour, plus extra for dusting

½ teaspoon baking powder

½ cup very finely chopped macadamia nuts

9 tablespoons unsalted butter, melted and cooled, plus extra for greasing

1. Place the eggs, sugar, maple syrup, and salt in a large bowl and beat with a handheld electric whisk until pale and thick, and doubled in volume. Sift in the flour and baking powder, then add the macadamia nuts and melted butter, and fold in until combined. Cover and chill for at least 10 minutes. (This helps the traditional "bump" to form in the center of each madeleine.)

2. Meanwhile, grease 18 holes of two 12-hole madeleine pans with melted butter, then dust lightly with flour, tapping the pans to remove any excess.

3. Gently stir the madeleine mixture, then spoon into the prepared pans until each hole is about three-quarters full. Bake at 425°F for 3 minutes, then reduce the oven temperature to 400°F and bake for an additional 4–6 minutes until risen and golden.

4. Transfer to a wire rack to cool slightly, then serve warm drizzled with extra warmed maple syrup, if desired.

# Charlotte Lucas's Mince Pies

This is a classic recipe that includes ground beef. You can omit this and add ¾ cup golden raisins and ½ cup brown sugar to the brandy mixture instead. It's important to let the fruit and spices steep in the brandy overnight to let the flavors develop.

---

*I*n Pride and Prejudice, *Mrs. Bennet tries to put down Charlotte Lucas, a possible rival to her daughters in the pursuit of Mr. Bingley, by implying that she has a close hand in the domestic affairs of the Lucas household:*

> *"Did Charlotte dine with you?"*

> *"No, she would go home. I fancy she was wanted about the mince-pies. For my part, Mr. Bingley, I always keep servants that can do their own work; my daughters are brought up very differently."*

*Mrs. Bennet's association of Charlotte with something so commonplace and particular as mince pies is exactly gauged to set the Lucases—Sir William Lucas is a baronet, Mr. Bennet merely a gentleman—down a peg or two. Austen, however, is also telling us something about Charlotte, who, if she is overseeing the making of the mince pies, is showing the same unsentimental shrewdness that leads her to accept the intolerable Mr. Collins as her marriage partner.*

*Packed with dried fruit and spice, mince pies were a staple in any respectable Regency household, eaten through the winter and not just at Christmas. By this period, too, they were usually made without the addition of the meat characteristic of medieval versions.*

Continued ↪

## MAKES 24

PREP + COOKING TIME: 45 MINUTES,
PLUS CHILLING

*For the filling*

scant ½ cup brandy

¾ cup currants

¾ cup raisins

¼ cup chopped preserved ginger

grated zest of ½ orange

grated zest of ½ lemon

½ teaspoon pumpkin pie spice

½ teaspoon grated nutmeg

½ cup chopped blanched almonds

7 oz. extra-lean ground beef

½ cup shredded suet

1 tart dessert apple, cored and grated

*For the pastry*

1¾ cups all-purpose flour, plus extra
    for dusting

pinch of salt

1 stick butter, diced

2½–3 tablespoons cold water

beaten egg, to glaze

sifted confectioners' sugar, for dusting

1. Make the filling. Pour the brandy into a saucepan, bring just to a boil, then add the dried fruits, ginger, fruit zest, and spices and leave to cool. Mix in the almonds, ground beef, suet, and apple, then cover and leave in the refrigerator overnight.

2. Next day, make the pastry. Add the flour and a pinch of salt to a large mixing bowl. Add the butter and rub into the flour with your fingertips until the mixture resembles fine crumbs. Gradually mix in just enough water to enable the crumbs to be squeezed together to form a soft but not sticky dough. Knead very gently until smooth.

3. Roll out two-thirds of the pastry on a lightly floured surface and stamp out twenty-four 3-inch circles with a cookie cutter. Press into the buttered sections of two 12-section muffin pans, rerolling the pastry as needed. Spoon in the filling.

4. Add any pastry trimmings to the reserved pastry, then roll out and stamp out twenty-four 2½-inch circles for the pie tops, rerolling the trimmings as needed. Brush the edges of the filled pie bases with beaten egg, add the lids, and press the edges together well.

5. Brush the tops with beaten egg, then make four small steam vents in each. Bake at 375°F for 15 minutes until the pastry is golden. Leave to stand for 10 minutes, then loosen and transfer to a wire rack to cool. Just before serving, dust the tops lightly with sifted confectioners' sugar.

# Cookbooks and Receipt Books

In Great Britain, the eighteenth century saw the rise of not only the novel but also the cookbook—two key genres of the century's burgeoning publishing industry. Both novels and cookbooks were bought largely by middle-class women, who were increasingly confined to the domestic sphere and to an enforced life of leisure. Who else would have the time to read the almost one million words of Clarissa; or, The History of a Young Lady (1748), the best-selling novel in letters by Samuel Richardson, still being read with enthusiasm by Jane Austen more than four decades later?

Almost contemporary with Clarissa was The Art of Cookery Made Plain and Easy (1747) by Hannah Glasse (1708–70). This was the best-selling cookbook of the century: by 1800 it had gone through no fewer than twenty editions. No respectable household—the Austens' included—would have been without a copy—used by the mistress of the house, not so much to cook herself as to give orders and ideas to the servants in the kitchen.

In terms of recipes, Glasse's cookbook was not especially revolutionary—a good third of them she compiled or purloined from other sources. There were some "firsts"—the first English recipe for a curry, the first for a trifle with gelatin, and so on—but what made the cookbook truly innovative was the straightforward, direct language Glasse used—as "plain and easy" as the title claimed. This was above all a practical kitchen guide for everyday use. This was especially important as cooks and kitchen maids were often illiterate, so the mistress would have to read out the recipes to them in the morning. Glasse's best-seller set the tone for the cookbooks that followed—even far into the nineteenth century, when Isabelle Beeton's Mrs. Beeton's Book of Household Management (1861) was very much in the Glasse tradition.

Published cookbooks, successful and ubiquitous as they became, did not supplant the other great tradition when it came to recipes, the handwritten household receipt book—a family collection that might be gathered over years, its entries begged and borrowed or evolved by a process of loving trial and error. Even quite grand ladies kept such books, but they were especially prevalent in more modest households, where it was never quite out of the question that the mistress and her daughters would have to roll up their sleeves, don aprons, and set about kneading dough or making jelly.

Such was very much the case in the Chawton household where Mrs. Austen and her daughters had not quite servants enough to escape kitchen chores. Indeed, there is rather the sense from Jane Austen's letters as well as her novels that she herself positively enjoyed getting involved in the nitty-gritty of food preparation, appraising the quality of a black butter, a sauce, or a pudding with a practiced eye. We are even lucky enough to have a receipt book from the Chawton household— compiled by the sisters' longtime friend and de facto housekeeper, Martha Lloyd (1765–1843), later Lady Francis Austen.

Lloyd's cookbook is now receiving the attention it deserves—for the brilliant snapshot it provides into Regency home cooking. In the Chawton household, we now realize, novels and cookbooks went ever hand in hand.

# Entertaining:

## Routs
## & Balls

*T*he Georgians loved to entertain and be entertained: dinner parties, card parties, routs, and balls, as well as gatherings in assembly rooms at watering-places like Bath and, on a smaller scale, in the inns of country towns, punctuated the social calendar. Here were opportunities for all, especially the young, to show off and be showed off to—and, with any luck, meet a suitable marriage partner. Appearance, clothes, manners, conversation, and accomplishments were all on display and subject to judgment—as Elizabeth Bennet discovers to her mortification in Pride and Prejudice, when she comes under the exacting gaze of Mr. Darcy.

The quintessential Jane Austen scene is the ball—held at the local assembly room or the ballroom of a large private house. For everyone in a neighborhood, a ball was a much anticipated affair and—like the cotillons, waltzes, and quadrilles danced there—were a peculiar combination of the highly formal and the erotically charged. It was the one great chance for the young to appraise one another, to flirt and get to know each other. Being a good dancer was a sign of a promising marriage partner, in both men and women.

Regency balls could last a long time, starting at nine o'clock in the evening and not finishing until three or even later in the morning. Refreshments, then—including quite a large amount of alcohol—were a necessity if the Mr. Bingleys and Miss Bennets of the world were to carry on dancing and getting to know one another.

While modern entertainments are likely to be less lavish or ambitious in scale, the following recipes will still conjure something of the romance and glamour of Mr. Bingley's Netherfield ball.

# Rout Cakes

These light and fruity little cakes are great for children to make—and eat!—as they are so quick and simple. These are best eaten on the day they are made, and are especially good still warm from the oven.

---

*I*n Emma, Mrs. Elton is much dissatisfied with the quality of the rout cakes served up at the Highbury card parties—by which she means, of course, that she is unhappy with society there, period. Mrs. Elton's specific complaint, however, may have arisen because of the rather uncertain identity of the "cakes" themselves—were they even a cake at all but rather more like a cookie? Did they have currants or not? The nearest contemporary recipe we have, from A New System of Domestic Cookery (1824), calls for quite a few flavorings—rosewater, orange-flower water, sweet wine, and brandy—in addition to the currants. Other nineteenth-century recipes called for them to be made into fancy shapes.

*Rout cakes, then, seem to have been something of a generic term for any sweet baked morsel served at a "rout," or party. Here is our take on them—deep-golden buttery spiced cookies studded with gleaming raisins. If you really want to go full-out Regency, pile them into a pyramid or in the shape of the Great Sphinx (Egyptomania was quite the thing)!*

## MAKES 18–20

PREP + COOKING TIME: **35** MINUTES

½ cup butter, softened

½ cup turbinado sugar, plus extra for sprinkling

1¾ cups self-rising flour

2 teaspoons pumpkin pie spice

1 egg

⅔ cup buttermilk

1¼ cups raisins

1. Beat the butter and sugar in a bowl until light and fluffy. Add the remaining ingredients and mix until evenly combined.

2. Using two forks, place small heaps of the mixture, spaced slightly apart, on two greased cookie sheets. Sprinkle with the extra sugar.

3. Bake at 375°F for 15–20 minutes or until deep golden, then transfer to a wire rack to cool.

# Fanny Price's Rose Garden Delights

These little rosewater-infused cakes are studded with chunks of Turkish delight and have a delicate floral flavor. If you can't find edible rose petals to decorate, chopped pistachios are a lovely topping too.

---

*The breeding of garden roses became something of a horticultural passion in eighteenth-century England, and by 1828 it was recorded that there were some 2,500 varieties. Unlike the long-flowering kinds of today, the roses of Jane Austen's garden at Chawton would have taken the form of tall, somewhat straggling shrubs, and would have flowered in one extravagant blooming in midsummer.*

*Given the importance of rosewater in the Georgian household, the cutting and drying of roses was one of the important tasks of the summer garden. In Mansfield Park, the put-upon heroine Fanny Price is given the Cinderella-like job of cutting roses in the full heat of the day, then taking them across the park to be dried in her Aunt Norris's home.*

*Here is another recipe using the rosewater of which the Georgians were so passionately fond (see the Rose-scented Fruit Salad on page 66). Serve sprinkled with chopped rose petals for an extra touch of Regency romance.*

*Continued* ⇝

## MAKES 18

PREP + COOKING TIME: **25** MINUTES

¾ cup unsalted butter, melted and
    cooled, plus extra for greasing
3 large egg whites
pinch of salt
1 cup almond flour
¾ cup all-purpose flour, sifted
¾ cup superfine sugar
1 teaspoon rosewater
5–7 pieces (3 oz.) rose-flavored
    Turkish delight, chopped
edible rose petals, to decorate

*For the rosewater cream*

scant 1 cup heavy cream
1 teaspoon rosewater
½ teaspoon vanilla bean paste or
    extract
¼ cup confectioners' sugar, sifted

1. Lightly brush 18 holes of two 12-hole madeleine pans or mini muffin pans with melted butter.

2. Whisk the egg whites and salt in a large, clean bowl with a handheld electric whisk until they form soft peaks, then gently fold in the almond flour, all-purpose flour, and sugar. Fold in the melted butter, rosewater, and Turkish delight.

3. Spoon the mixture into the prepared pans and bake at 425°F for 8–10 minutes until risen and golden.

4. Meanwhile, make the rosewater cream. Whip all the ingredients in a bowl with a handheld electric whisk until soft peaks form, then place in a serving bowl.

5. Remove the cakes from the oven and transfer to a wire rack to cool slightly. Serve with dollops of the rosewater cream and decorated with edible rose petals.

# Steventon Tiny Treacle Tarts

This classic British dessert with its crumbly pastry and gooey, lemon-infused filling has been reinvented in miniature. Serve these dainty treats warm with spoonfuls of whipped cream sprinkled with ground cinnamon, or with vanilla ice cream.

———————————————————

*While the first recipe for treacle tarts properly dates only to the late nineteenth century—when the amber-colored treacle known as "golden syrup" was invented—there are recipes for similar tarts filled with sugary, buttery, spiced mixtures from much earlier. In the seventeenth century, for example, we find a "sweetmeat cake"—a tart filled with candied orange peel, butter, and sugar. In any case, we can well imagine something of this ilk served in Reverend Austen's household in the Steventon parsonage—the perfect pudding for his large, growing family, especially when served with a big jug of thick, cold cream.*

## MAKES 24

PREP + COOKING TIME: 45 MINUTES,
  PLUS CHILLING

generous ½ cup all-purpose flour
scant ⅓ cup confectioners' sugar
7 tablespoons butter, diced
2 egg yolks

*For the filling*

3½ tablespoons butter
½ cup brown sugar
generous ¾ cup light corn syrup
grated zest of 1 lemon
2 tablespoons lemon juice
1 egg, beaten
1 cup fresh bread crumbs

1. To make the pastry, add the flour, confectioners' sugar, and butter to a food processor or mixing bowl and mix until you have fine crumbs. Add the egg yolks and mix together until you have a soft ball. Wrap in plastic wrap and chill for 15 minutes.

2. Roll out the pastry thinly on a lightly floured surface, then stamp out twenty-four 2½-inch circles with a fluted cookie cutter and press into the buttered sections of two 12-section mini muffin pans. Reknead and reroll pastry trimmings as needed. Chill for 15 minutes.

3. Put the butter, sugar, syrup, lemon zest, and juice in a small saucepan and cook over a low heat until the butter has just melted and the sugar has dissolved. Take off the heat and leave to cool slightly.

4. Stir the beaten egg and bread crumbs into the syrup mix and beat until smooth. Spoon into the pastry cases.

5. Bake at 350°F for 15–20 minutes. Leave to cool for 15 minutes, then loosen the tarts with a knife and remove from the tins. Transfer to a wire rack and leave to cool slightly.

# Mrs. Jennings's Shortcakes

These mini orange shortcakes are perfect for a party. To make a lemony version, replace the orange zest with lemon zest and dust over 2 teaspoons of superfine sugar mixed with finely grated zest of half a lemon to serve.

---

*O*ne of the institutions of the Georgian household was the evening "tea tray." With dinner eaten quite early, even in fashionable houses, an evening spent in quiet occupations or entertaining friends in the drawing room was broken by the arrival of not just tea but a light collation of cakes, cookies, savories, and fruits, spread out over a small table.

In Sense and Sensibility, *such tea trays seem to be especially popular in the London home of the kindly, if slightly vulgar, Mrs. Jennings, with whom Elinor and Marianne have been invited to stay. The tea things have just been brought in when Marianne, pining for her fiancé, Willoughby—who inexplicably has not yet paid her a visit—is startled by a loud knock at the door. She is sure it is Willoughby . . . it must be . . . but no, it is "only" Colonel Brandon, her other, despised suitor.*

*The romantic Marianne, who straightaway rushes out of the room, may have been too distracted to notice the buttery shortcakes set out on the tea table, but sensible Elinor would surely have the presence of mind to offer one to the poor perturbed colonel.*

## MAKES ABOUT 80

PREP + COOKING TIME: 22 MINUTES

2 cups all-purpose flour, sifted

¾ cup plus 2 tablespoons butter,
    chilled and diced

grated zest of 1 orange

½ teaspoon pumpkin pie spice

⅓ cup superfine sugar

2 teaspoons cold water

*To serve*

2 teaspoons confectioners' sugar

1 teaspoon cocoa powder

1. Put the flour in a bowl or food processor. Add the butter and rub in with your fingertips or process until the mixture resembles fine bread crumbs. Add the remaining ingredients with the measured water and mix or blend to a dough.

2. Roll out the dough on a lightly floured surface to ⅛ inch thick. Cut out about 80 rounds using a ¾-inch cookie cutter, rerolling the trimmings to make more. Place on two large cookie sheets lined with parchment paper.

3. Bake at 400°F for 10–12 minutes until golden. Transfer to a wire rack to cool.

4. Sift together the confectioners' sugar and cocoa powder and dust a little over the cookies before serving.

# Negus

Ideal for winter celebrations of all kinds, the delicious smell of cloves and cinnamon will fill the air when you make this cheering drink. There's no need to splurge on the wine—any inexpensive bottle will be fine.

---

The Watsons—*Jane Austen's (very) unfinished novel begun in 1803 and set aside in 1805—begins with "the first winter assembly in the town of D. in Surrey." As with most country assemblies, this is held in the local coaching inn, which had a large upstairs room set aside for the purpose. One of the beaus of the ball is the "irresistible" Tom Musgrave—an incorrigible flirt with whom all the young women dream of dancing—but whom the novel's heroine, the newcomer-in-town Emma Watson, coolly turns down when he asks her to dance. Peeved, he skulks away, and the narrator asks us to "imagine him mortifying with his barrel of oysters in dreary solitude, or gladly assisting the landlady in her bar to make fresh negus for the happy dancers above."*

*Negus—mulled wine or port—was a popular party drink through the eighteenth and nineteenth centuries, named for and perhaps invented by English army officer Colonel Francis Negus (1670–1732).*

## SERVES 6

PREP + COOKING TIME: 25 MINUTES

1 bottle red wine
1¼ cups apple juice
1¼ cups water
juice of 1 orange
1 orange, sliced
½ lemon, sliced
1 cinnamon stick, halved
6 cloves
2 bay leaves
½ cup superfine sugar
⅔ cup brandy

1. Pour the wine, apple juice, measured water, and orange juice into a large saucepan.

2. Add the sliced orange and lemon, the cinnamon stick, cloves, and bay leaves, then mix in the sugar and brandy.

3. Cover with a lid and simmer for at least 20 minutes, until piping hot. The longer it simmers, the more the flavors will develop. Ladle into heatproof glasses to serve.

# Mrs. Allen's Tea Punch

With its wonderful scent of citrus combined with mint, this refreshing iced tea is a lovely way to stay hydrated and refreshed on a hot day. Just pour a tall glass, pull up a deck chair, and relax under the cool shade of a tree.

---

*T*ea *was the regular refreshment served at a Regency assembly or ball, served in a room adjoining the ballroom in between the dance sets. This was taken sitting down, and served from large silver tea urns. Decorum dictated that men should fetch the tea, so women, if unattended, might be left without refreshment. This occurs in* Northanger Abbey, *when Catherine Morland and her chaperone, Mrs. Allen, finally manage to squeeze themselves into two places at a tea table at the Bath Assembly Rooms. Catherine is overwhelmed with social embarrassment:*

> *"What shall we do? The gentlemen and ladies at this table look as if they wondered why we came here—we seem forcing ourselves into their party."*
> *"Aye, so we do. That is very disagreeable. I wish we had a large acquaintance here."*
> *"I wish we had any—it would be somebody to go to."*
> *"Very true, my dear; and if we knew anybody we would join them directly . . ."*
> *"Had not we better go away as it is? Here are no tea-things for us, you see."*

*In the best of all possible worlds, Catherine and Mrs. Allen might have promptly been served with a glass of tea punch, made all the more refreshing by the addition of mint—the perfect antidote to the heat and crowds of the Assembly Rooms.*

## SERVES 4

PREP + COOKING TIME: 20 MINUTES,
PLUS COOLING AND CHILLING

large bunch of peppermint, spearmint,
   and garden mint, leaves picked
2 oranges, plus orange slices, to
   decorate
2 tablespoons green tea leaves
¼ cup sugar, to taste
juice of 1 lime, plus lime slices,
   to decorate
crushed ice, to serve

1. Using a mortar and pestle, bruise the peppermint,
   spearmint, and garden mint leaves with 2 tablespoons
   of the sugar. Add the sliced zest of 1 orange and bruise
   to release the flavors.

2. Tip the mixture into a heavy-based saucepan, add
   the green tea leaves, the remaining sugar, and 2½
   cups water, and bring to a boil, stirring continuously
   until the sugar has dissolved. Reduce the heat and
   simmer for 2–3 minutes.

3. Stir in the juice of both oranges and the lime juice.
   Leave to cool in the pan. Strain into a pitcher and
   chill in the freezer for 10–15 minutes.

4. To serve, fill four tall glasses with crushed ice, pour
   in the chilled tea, and decorate each with a slice of
   orange and a slice of lime.

# Champagne Ice

Served in elegant glasses, this is a sophisticated and light dessert to end a special meal. For a more pocket-friendly version, prosecco is a great alternative to champagne. The granita melts quickly so, if you can, chill the glasses you're planning to serve it in.

---

*W*ealthy Georgians began to fall in love with sparkling champagne through the eighteenth century. The Napoleonic Wars (1802–15) and the associated naval blockades at the beginning of the nineteenth century may have hampered the wine trade and the love affair, but some lavishly expensive bottles still reached the London elite. Beau Brummell (1778–1840)—an iconic figure of the Regency—is even said to have recommended having one's boots cleaned with champagne.

*This beautiful granita makes far better use of this bubbly extravagance (though feel free to substitute it with another sparkling wine of your choice). Imagine it served in little crystal glasses at a select party given by the Prince Regent (later George IV) in his exotic pleasure palace by the sea—the Royal Pavilion in Brighton.*

*The Prince Regent was a great admirer of Jane Austen's work, having a set of her novels in each of his palaces. So, in an alternative world, we might imagine the novelist as a guest of honor at the Royal Pavilion party, supping on this delectable ice—were it not for the fact that Austen loathed him, mostly out of solidarity with his long-suffering wife, Caroline of Brunswick.*

## SERVES 6

PREP + COOKING TIME: **25** MINUTES, PLUS COOLING AND FREEZING

3 tablespoons sugar

⅔ cup boiling water

1⅔ cups medium dry champagne

1½ cups raspberries

1. Stir the sugar into the measured water until it has dissolved, then leave to cool.

2. Mix together the sugar syrup and champagne. Pour it into a shallow, nonstick baking pan so that it is no more than 1 inch deep.

3. Freeze the mixture for 2 hours until it is mushy, then break up the ice crystals with a fork. Return the mixture to the freezer for an additional 2 hours, beating every 30 minutes until it has formed fine, icy flakes.

4. Spoon the granita into glasses and top with the raspberries.

# Lydia Bennet's Orgeat

An essential ingredient in a mai tai and other cocktails, this marzipan-like syrup is also good splashed into coffee, diluted in sparkling water, or drizzled over ice cream. You can ring the changes by swapping rosewater for the orange flower water.

———————————

*O*ne of the nonalcoholic drinks on offer as a refreshment to the tired dancers at the Netherfield ball may well have been the sweet almond-flavored drink known as orgeat. Originally made from barley (from the French word for the grain, orge), by Georgian times orgeat had become a thick, creamy mixture made with pounded bitter almonds, rosewater or orange flower water, and plenty of sugar syrup. Just a tablespoonful was added to a glass of water for a refreshing, restorative drink.

*No doubt the frivolous Lydia Bennet, with her "high animal spirits," would have preferred this alcoholic version, finding in it the reinvigoration she needs as she sets off to dance with yet another of the Meryton officers.*

## MAKES 1 SMALL BOTTLE

PREP + COOKING TIME: 15 MINUTES,
    PLUS STANDING TIME

2 cups blanched almonds
1¼ cups water
1½ cups sugar
¼ cup vodka or brandy
1 teaspoon orange flower water

1. Place the almonds in a food processor or blender and blitz until coarsely ground, then set aside.

2. Put the measured water and sugar in a saucepan over a medium heat and stir until the sugar dissolves. Bring to a boil and allow to boil for 3 minutes before adding the ground almonds.

3. Simmer on a low heat for 3 minutes and just before the mixture comes to a boil, remove from the heat. Cover and set aside for 3–8 hours.

4. Line a strainer with two layers of clean cheesecloth and strain the mixture, pressing to extract as much of the liquid as possible. Discard the ground almonds.

5. Stir in the vodka or brandy and orange flower water and, using a funnel, pour into a clean glass bottle.

6. Seal and store in the refrigerator for up to 2 weeks.

# Admiral Croft's "Great Comet" Grog

Enjoy this spiced brandy-based ratafia on its own over ice cubes, or mix one part ratafia to five parts sparkling wine or sparkling water. It's strong, so a little goes a long way!

---

*T*hrough the final months of 1811 a brilliant comet became visible in the evening sky and astronomers and ordinary folk alike gathered to observe its spectacular progress across the heavens. This "Great Comet" became a sensation, its appearance commemorated in the art and literature of the time, as well as in diaries and notebooks. As is often the case with the so-called great comets, the 1811 comet was also associated (unscientifically) with the year's especially good vintage of wine and brandies, though the 1811 great comet vintage was long the best remembered.

*We do not know whether Jane watched the comet from her garden at Chawton that year (perhaps she was just too busy writing* Emma*). Here, however, we have imagined a celebratory brandy-laced drink invented by one of her most gregarious characters,* Persuasion's *Admiral Croft, after he and his wife have watched the comet from the deck of his ship while out at sea. Every year after, they celebrate the event—and their long, happy marriage—by making the drink using the famous 1811 Great Comet brandy and serving it up to friends and family, including, of course, the newlyweds Frederick and Anne Wentworth.*

## MAKES 1–2 BOTTLES

PREP TIME: **20** MINUTES

3 cups brandy

½ cup sugar

1 cinnamon stick

1 strip lemon peel

2 strips orange peel

2 cups cherries, pitted and lightly crushed

2 cups blackberries

3 cloves, bruised

1 cardamom pod, crushed

1. Put all the ingredients in a large sealable jar and stir well. Seal and leave in a cool, dark place for a month. Shake the jar once a week.

2. Strain through cheesecloth, pressing hard on the fruit and spices, and decant into sterilized bottles.

# Assemblies, Routs, and Balls

---

*Entertaining—from casual visits, through card parties and dinners, to the balls held in large private homes and the gatherings and dances of the assembly rooms of town and country—is the lynchpin of Jane Austen's novels. Such events, ranging across the whole gamut from the informal and unexpected—a friend or relative dropping by as Mr. Knightley does near the beginning of* Emma*—to the formal and much anticipated—such as the Netherfield ball in* Pride and Prejudice*—form the necessary backdrop for both the social comedy and unfurling romance. Conversation is key, as are music and dance, but also food and drink: friendships and marriages are made or lost over tea trays, alliances and enmities forged at a picnic, misunderstandings fallen into over the card table or by the fortepiano . . .*

*It was the private balls and assemblies that formed the apex of the entertainment culture of Regency Britain as well as in Austen's fictional world. From around the mid-eighteenth century, assembly rooms were built in large towns and cities the length and breadth of the country, their grandiose Neoclassical architecture a matter of much local pride. Assemblies were held perhaps monthly through the fall and winter months—a season of gatherings for which attendees paid a subscription. A master of ceremonies ruled over assemblies with a fist of iron, velvet-covered naturally—making sure only the "quality" attended and that the dress code and other points of etiquette were followed, and, where appropriate, making introductions between newcomers and strangers. There were usually three main rooms: the ballroom itself, whose lengths were lined with chairs for spectators; a card room; and a supper room where tea and other drinks were laid out on tables. Sometimes there was a billiards room, too, for the older, married gentlemen whose dancing days were over.*

*The most famous and grandest assembly rooms of all, of course, were at Bath, which feature in both* Persuasion *and* Northanger Abbey*. This venue, designed by John Wood the Younger as part of the larger Bath complex of residential streets, squares, and circuses, was first opened to* the public in 1771. In the description of Catherine Morland's first visit to the Bath Assembly Rooms—perhaps reflecting Austen's own first impressions— it is the unbearable number of people crammed into its rooms that strike both the heroine and the reader:

> The season was full, the room crowded, and the two ladies squeezed in as well as they could . . . Mrs. Allen made her way through the throng of men by the door, as swiftly as the necessary caution would allow; Catherine, however, kept close at her side, and linked her arm too firmly within her friend's to be torn asunder by any common effort of a struggling assembly . . . By unwearied diligence they gained even the top of the room, their situation was just the same; they saw nothing of the dancers but the high feathers of some of the ladies . . .
>
> Everybody was shortly in motion for tea, and they must squeeze out like the rest. Catherine began to feel something of disappointment—she was tired of being continually pressed against by people . . . with all of whom she was so wholly unacquainted that she could not relieve the irksomeness of imprisonment by the exchange of a syllable with any of her fellow captives.

Given this unpleasant, not to say claustrophobic, description, it is no wonder that the word "rout"—usually applied to a disorderly retreat of soldiers—came to be applied to such society gatherings, at once so rigorously controlled and wildly unrestrained.

All in all, the smaller, quieter town assemblies—held in the large upper rooms of inns and altogether more informal in tone—sound much more appealing, and were certainly so to Austen, for whom human intimacy and warmth were always more important than grandeur and fashion. The small-town Meryton assembly depicted near the beginning of Pride and Prejudice may well arouse the London snobbishness of some of the Netherfield party— Caroline Bingley and Mr. Darcy among them—but Jane Austen's sympathies are all with the frank and natural enjoyment of the local inhabitants at play.

# Index

## A

Admiral Croft's "Great Comet" grog 155
almond flour: Fanny Price's rose garden
  delights 143–4
  Martha Lloyd's ratafia cakes 126
almonds: Charlotte Lucas's mince pies
  135–7
  cherry almond ice cream 120–1
  Lydia Bennet's orgeat 154
apple juice: negus 149
apples: Mr. Woodhouse's "all-apple" tarts
  116
arugula leaves: Mary Musgrove's meat
  platter 52
asparagus: Cassandra's lobster and
  asparagus 83
  Chawton Cottage garden risotto 99
  Lyme Bay mackerel 80
  Mrs. Cassandra Austen's scrambled
  eggs 13
assemblies, routs, and balls 156–7
avocado: club sandwich 56

## B

bacon: club sandwich 56
  Mansfield wood roast pheasant 85–6
  Mrs. Bennet's venison pot 90
Bath buns 22–3
beef: beef steak and caramelized leek
  sandwich 55
  Charlotte Lucas's mince pies 135–7
berries: summer berry delice 113–14
biscuits: Captain Frederick Wentworth's
  ship's biscuits 65
  strawberry and lavender shortcakes 68
blackberries: Admiral Croft's "Great
  Comet" grog 155
  Chawton Cottage plum pudding 127–8
Box Hill picnic pies 36–7
brandy: Admiral Croft's "Great Comet"
  grog 155
  Lydia Bennet's orgeat 154
bread: beef steak and caramelized leek
  sandwich 55
  club sandwich 56
  Henry Tilney's nice mushroom patties
  102–3
  Lady Catherine de Bourgh's caraway and
  raisin breakfast bread 24
  turkey, watercress, cranberry sauce, and
  mayo sandwiches 55
breakfast 8–31

brioche: Lady Susan's raspberry and
  mascarpone brioche 17
  love and friendship pain perdu 18
  Mary Crawford's tarragon & mushroom
  brioche 17
  Mrs. Cassandra Austen's scrambled
  eggs 13
buns, Bath 22–3

## C

cakes: Fanny Price's rose garden delights
  143–4
  gingerbread loaf 133
  Mrs. Weston's wedding cake 130–1
  pound cake 26–7
  rout cakes 142
Captain Frederick Wentworth's ship's
  biscuits 65
caraway and raisin breakfast bread, Lady
  Catherine de Bourgh's 24
cardamom coffee, Frank Churchill's 28
Cassandra's lobster and asparagus 83
cauliflower: a potato and cauliflower
  curry 100
champagne ice 152
Charlotte Lucas's mince pies 135–7
Chawton Cottage garden risotto 99
Chawton Cottage plum pudding 127–8
cheese: Cassandra's lobster and asparagus
  83
  Mary Musgrove's meat platter 52
  Mrs. Austen's spinach and potato gratin
  107
  perfect picnic parcels 40
cheesecakes, Devizes 125
cherries: Admiral Croft's "Great Comet"
  grog 155
  cherry almond ice cream 120–1
chestnuts: chestnut jelly with whisky 60
  Mrs. Bennet's venison pot 90
  Pemberley chestnut soup 50–1
chicken: chicken curry 88
  club sandwich 56
chicken stock: Netherfield white soup 77
chocolate: General Tilney's hot chocolate
  31
  Lydia's whim-wham 123
club sandwich 56
coffee, Frank Churchill's cardamom 28
Comtesse de Feuillide's breakfast brioches
  three ways 16–18
conserve, Donwell Abbey strawberry 21

cookbooks 138–9
cookies: Mrs. Jennings's shortcakes 148
cooler, William Cowper's poetical melon
  71
couscous: Lyme Bay mackerel 80
cranberry sauce: turkey, watercress,
  cranberry sauce, and mayo sandwiches
  55
cream: Fanny Price's rose garden delights
  143–4
  Lydia's whim-wham 123
  Mrs. Weston's wedding cake 130–1
  strawberry and lavender shortcakes 68
  whipt syllabub 112
cream cheese: Devizes cheesecakes 125
cucumber: salmagundi 78
curry: chicken curry 88
  potato and cauliflower curry 100
custard: Lydia's whim-wham 123

## D

delice, summer berry 113–14
Devizes cheesecakes 125
dinner 74–107
Donwell Abbey strawberry conserve 21
Dr. Grant's sandwich tray 54–6
dried fruit: Charlotte Lucas's mince pies
  135–7
drinks: Admiral Croft's "Great Comet"
  grog 155
  Frank Churchill's cardamom coffee 28
  General Tilney's hot chocolate 31
  Lydia Bennet's orgeat 154
  Mrs. Allen's tea punch 150–1
  Mrs. Morland's gingered pear juice 70
  negus 149
  William Cowper's poetical melon cooler
  71
duck, pear, and raspberry salad 46

## E

eggs: Henry Crawford's lazy breakfast
  eggs 10
  love and friendship pain perdu 18
  Mrs. Cassandra Austen's scrambled
  eggs 13
  Netherfield white soup 77
Elizabeth Martin's sausage rolls 38
entertaining 140–57

## F

Fanny Price's rose garden delights 143–4

**Picture Acknowledgments**

Dreamstime.com/Ekaterina Kolchenko
cover, 1, 3.  iStock/Daxi 8 (used
throughout).  Octopus Publishing Group/
Stephen Conroy 11, 20, 27, 37, 39, 59, 63,
64, 93, 106, 121, 122, 129, 136, 145, 147; Will
Heap 19, 28, 31, 45, 53, 89, 95, 114, 124, 132,
151; Lis Parsons 41, 42, 57, 81, 131; William
Shaw 13, 15, 25, 48, 51, 69, 76, 82, 87, 98,
101, 153; Ian Wallace 79, 103, 105, 117.